CW00959743

PREHISTORIC ·LIFE·

Written by
Steve Parker

Illustrated by
Sergio

DORLING KINDERSLEY • LONDON

DK

A Dorling Kindersley Book

Editor Miranda Smith
Art editor Chris Scollen
Designer Margo White

Art director Roger Priddy

Editorial consultant William Lindsay
Production Norina Bremner

First published in Great Britain in 1991 by Dorling Kindersley Limited, 9 Henrietta Street, London WC2E 8PS

A CIP catalogue record for this book is available from the British Library.

ISBN 0-86318-597-5

Colour Separations by DOT Gradations Limited
Printed in Spain by Artes Graficas, Toledo S. A.
D.L.TO:2419-1990

CONTENTS

FOSSIL FACTS

For centuries, people have been finding strange lumps of rock in the ground. Some looked like bones, while others resembled shells, or teeth, or bits of tree bark. Many people thought they were "accidents of nature", or the work of the gods - or devils! Gradually, over the past 200 years, it has been realized that these lumps of rock are the remains of long-dead animals and plants, which have been buried and slowly turned to stone. We call them fossils. The scientific study of fossils, and the rock layers which contain them, has revealed that life began many millions of years ago. It also shows that many animals and plants have appeared, lived for a time, and then died out.

Fossils through time

Scientists can measure the age of a rock in several ways. As a result, we know that during certain times in the Earth's history, certain kinds of animals and plants were alive. Over nine-tenths of them have died out for ever.

Trilobite

This creature was a sea-living relative of the crabs of today. Fossils found show that there were many thousands of kinds of trilobites. Their history began some 600 million years ago (pages 10-13).

Nautiloid

Cousins of the modern squid, nautiloids flourished in many sizes and shapes more than 500 million years ago (pages 10-13). Today, there is only one type that survives, the pearly nautilus.

PRECAMBRIAN ERA

Cambrian

Scientists have devised a timetable which divides the history of the Earth into eras. The eras in turn are divided into periods, and the periods into epochs. The longest span of time was the Precambrian era. This lasted from the beginning of the Earth, some 4,600 million years ago, to about 570 million years ago. During this time, life in the sea progressed from tiny blobs of floating jelly to the first complex creatures such as worms, jellyfishes and sea-pens.

570 mya

Animals with shells or other hard coverings had appeared in the seas. These included trilobites, graptolites and brachiopods (lampshells).

500 mya

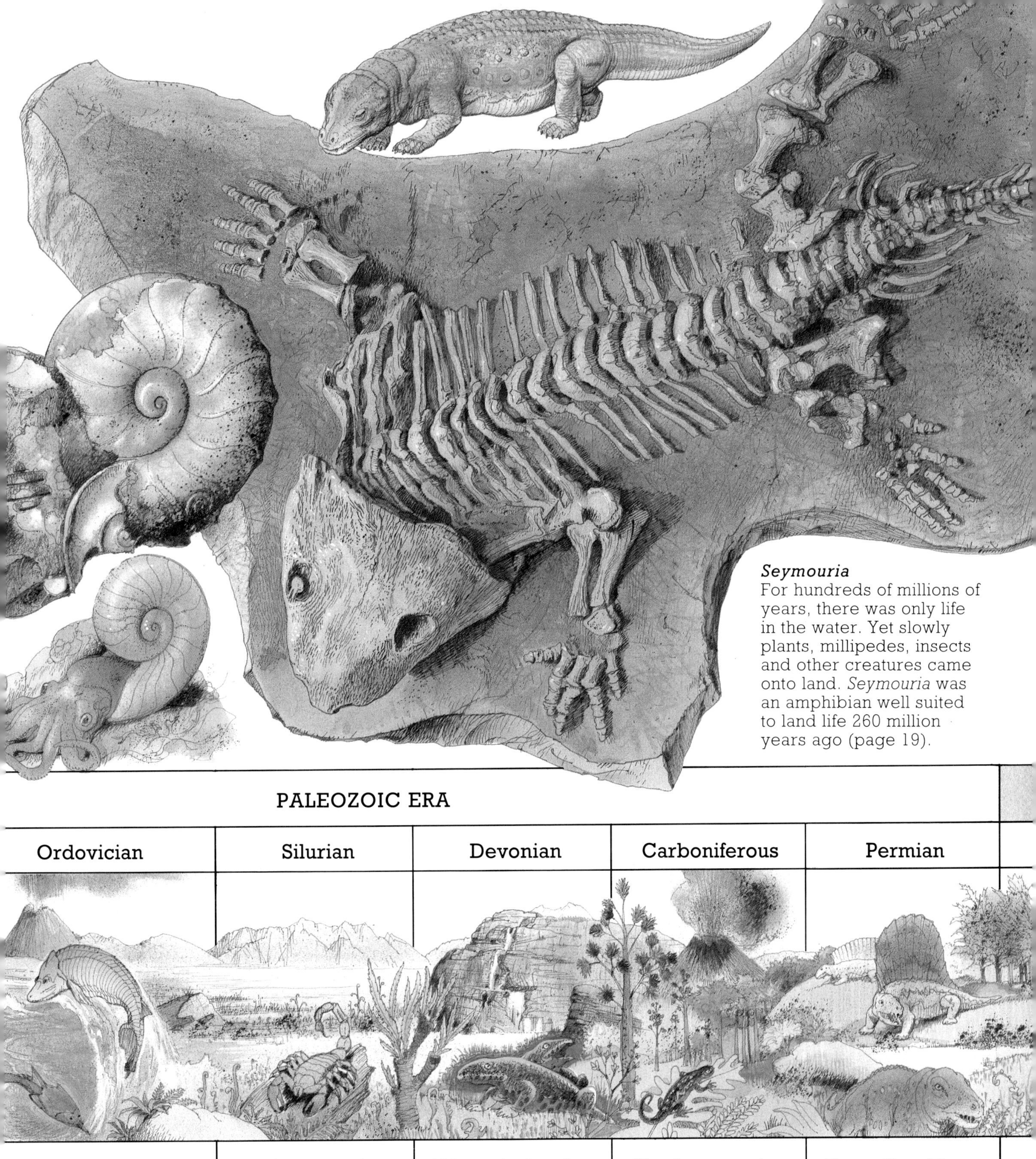

Seymouria
For hundreds of millions of years, there was only life in the water. Yet slowly plants, millipedes, insects and other creatures came onto land. *Seymouria* was an amphibian well suited to land life 260 million years ago (page 19).

PALEOZOIC ERA

Ordovician	Silurian	Devonian	Carboniferous	Permian
Coral animals built stony reefs in warm, shallow seas, and sea urchins developed. The first fishes appeared, but they had no fins or jaws.	Fish from several groups swam in the seas. Sea scorpions as big as people hunted. On land, the first small plants were beginning to grow.	This was the Age of Fishes, with sharks and many other kinds of fishes swarming in the seas. Insects and the first amphibians crawled out on land.	Giant ferns grew in steamy swamps, and giant amphibians hunted the giant dragonflies. The coal we use as fuel began to form at this time.	The reptiles of the Carboniferous period evolved into various groups and began to take over the land. Trilobites were fading from the sea.
430 mya	395 mya	345 mya	280 mya	225 mya

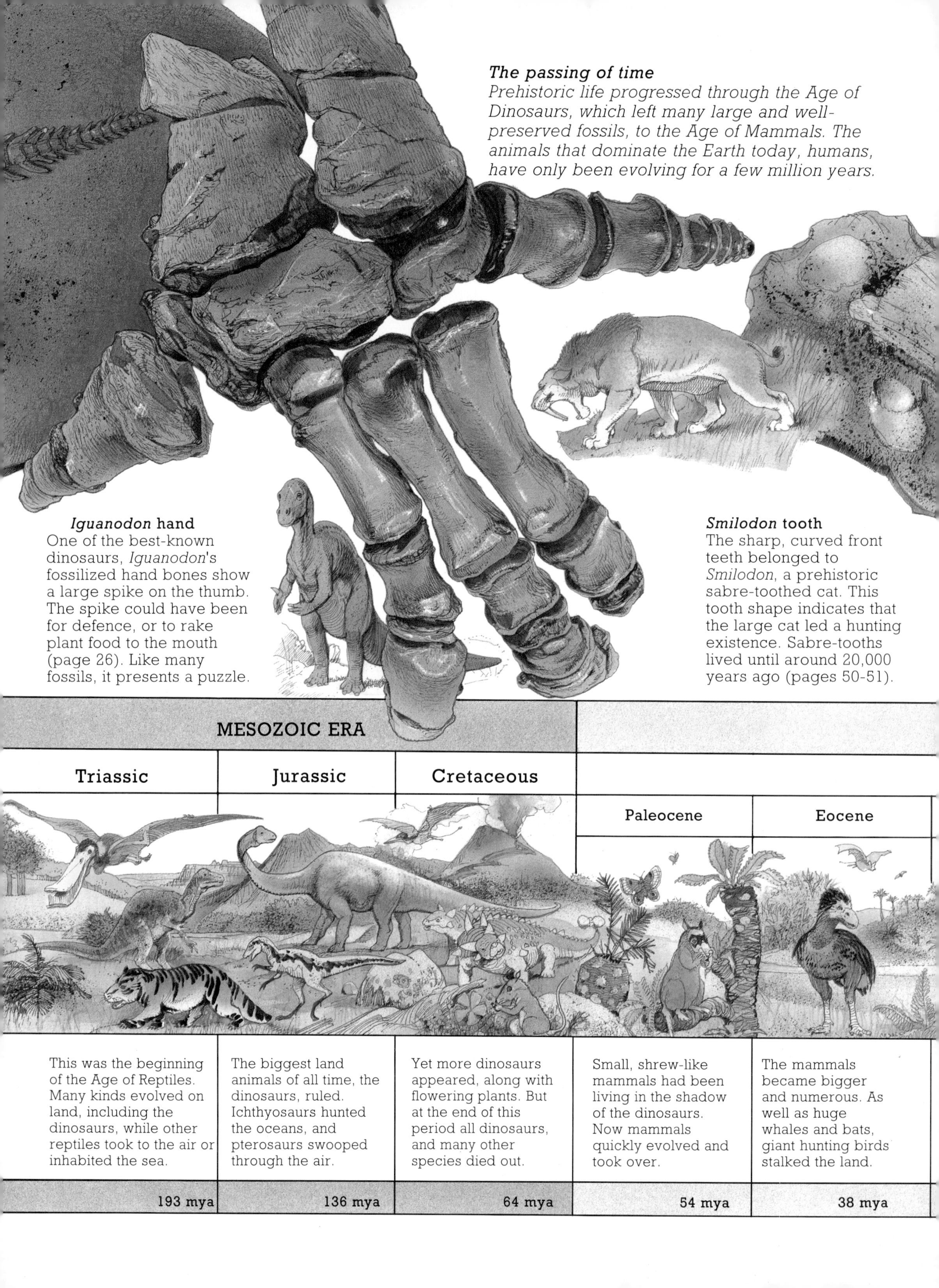

The passing of time
Prehistoric life progressed through the Age of Dinosaurs, which left many large and well-preserved fossils, to the Age of Mammals. The animals that dominate the Earth today, humans, have only been evolving for a few million years.

***Iguanodon* hand**
One of the best-known dinosaurs, *Iguanodon*'s fossilized hand bones show a large spike on the thumb. The spike could have been for defence, or to rake plant food to the mouth (page 26). Like many fossils, it presents a puzzle.

***Smilodon* tooth**
The sharp, curved front teeth belonged to *Smilodon*, a prehistoric sabre-toothed cat. This tooth shape indicates that the large cat led a hunting existence. Sabre-tooths lived until around 20,000 years ago (pages 50-51).

MESOZOIC ERA				
Triassic	Jurassic	Cretaceous		
			Paleocene	Eocene
This was the beginning of the Age of Reptiles. Many kinds evolved on land, including the dinosaurs, while other reptiles took to the air or inhabited the sea.	The biggest land animals of all time, the dinosaurs, ruled. Ichthyosaurs hunted the oceans, and pterosaurs swooped through the air.	Yet more dinosaurs appeared, along with flowering plants. But at the end of this period all dinosaurs, and many other species died out.	Small, shrew-like mammals had been living in the shadow of the dinosaurs. Now mammals quickly evolved and took over.	The mammals became bigger and numerous. As well as huge whales and bats, giant hunting birds stalked the land.
193 mya	136 mya	64 mya	54 mya	38 mya

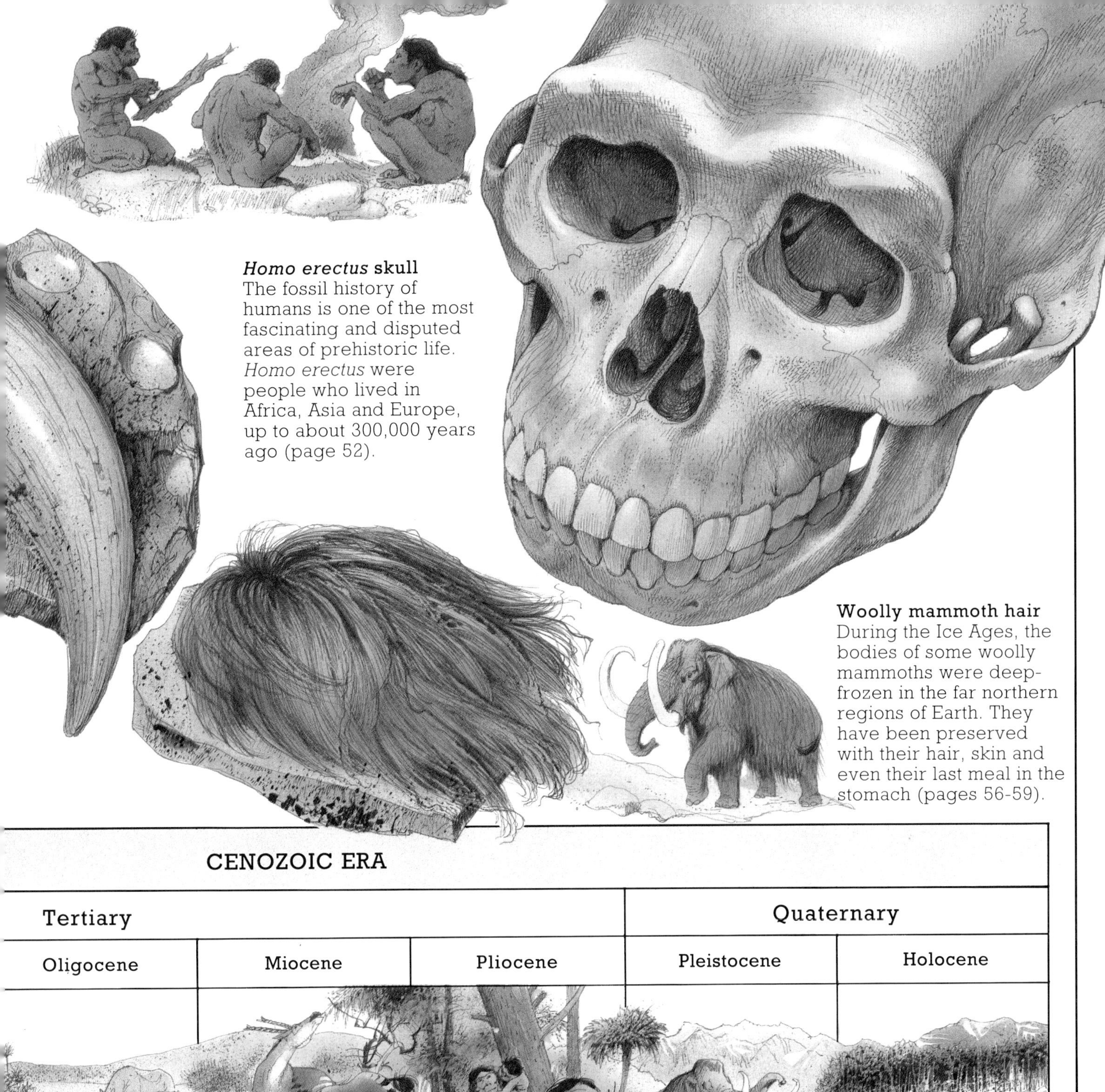

***Homo erectus* skull**
The fossil history of humans is one of the most fascinating and disputed areas of prehistoric life. *Homo erectus* were people who lived in Africa, Asia and Europe, up to about 300,000 years ago (page 52).

Woolly mammoth hair
During the Ice Ages, the bodies of some woolly mammoths were deep-frozen in the far northern regions of Earth. They have been preserved with their hair, skin and even their last meal in the stomach (pages 56-59).

CENOZOIC ERA				
Tertiary			Quaternary	
Oligocene	Miocene	Pliocene	Pleistocene	Holocene

Many modern mammals were now established, and the giant flightless birds and creodonts lost out on land.	As the climate became drier, forests shrank and grasslands spread. Deer, horses, rhinos and elephants fed among the trees and on the plains.	Many land creatures - insects, reptiles, birds and mammals - were similar to today's. In the sea, bony fishes had become the most important fish group.	During the Ice Ages, some mammals had thick fur coats to survive the cold. In Interglacial periods, tropical plants and animals moved north.	With the retreat of the last major ice sheets, the first villages and towns grew up in the Middle East area. Prehistory had ended; history was beginning.
26 mya	7 mya	2 mya	10,000 years ago	Today

HARD EVIDENCE

For hundreds of millions of years during the formation of the Earth, conditions were too extreme for life. There were poisonous gases in the atmosphere, volcanoes erupted and red-hot lava flowed on land. Slowly the planet's surface settled and the seas calmed. For it was in the sea, as far as we know, that life began. Its earliest signs are microscopic specks which could be simple bacteria-type life forms, in very ancient rocks. By about 3,500 million years ago the rocks show the ring-shaped fossils of stromatolites, which are circular, mat-like growths of organisms called blue-green algae in shallow seas. The first fossils of simple animals and plants date from about 700 million years ago, although they may have appeared before this.

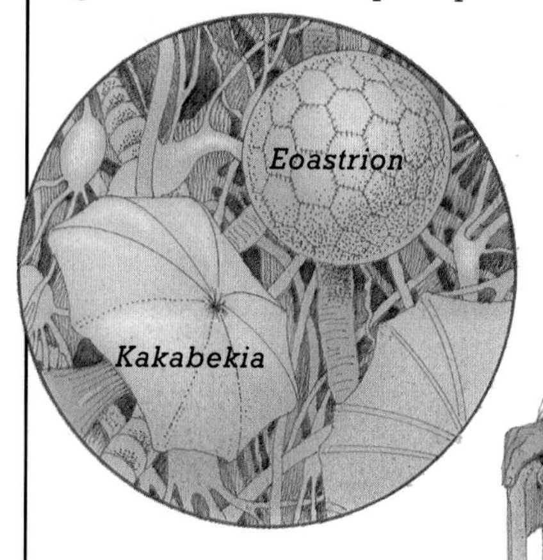

Gunflint microfossils
Under the microscope, certain rocks 2,000 million years old show tiny fossils of one-celled life forms. The umbrella-shaped *Kakabekia* and branching *Eoastrion* were found first in chert rocks at Gunflint in Canada.

Ostracods
Distant relations of crabs and barnacles, each ostracod has a hinged two-part shell. Some fossils are used by scientists as examples, or indicators, of a particular period of time. The changing shell patterns of ostracods make them good indicators.

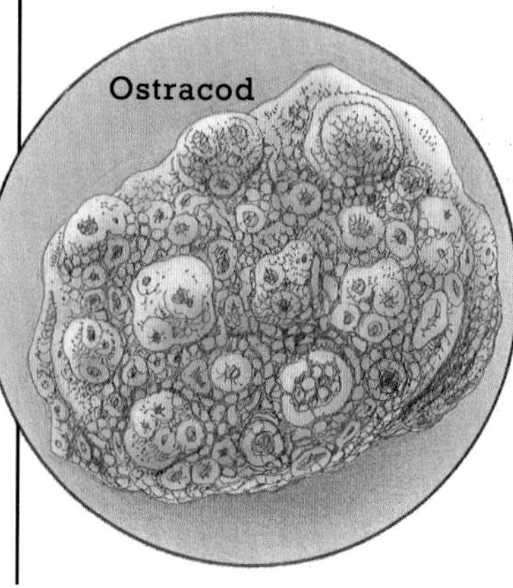

Foraminiferans
Billions of these one-celled organisms lived 600 million years ago, and they still thrive in oceans today. Their hard, beautifully sculpted shells have fossilized and built up into thick layers of rock.

Foraminiferans

Rock types
Of the three main kinds of rock - metamorphic, igneous and sedimentary - only the last may contain fossils. Sedimentary rocks are formed from sand, silt, mud and other particles that collect on the beds of rivers, lakes and seas.

Ostracods have existed since Cambrian times, their fossilized shells abundant in some rocks

Unravelling the record in the rocks

Only a tiny proportion of animals and plants are preserved as fossils - the rest rot away and leave no trace. Likewise, only a few of the many kinds of rocks contain fossils. Therefore, finding fossils takes know-how and also a good slice of luck. The fossils of early life are difficult to study, because they are usually faint and distorted.

Blue-green algae

Along with bacteria, blue-green algae are among the simplest living things and some of the first to evolve. (Their other name is cyanobacteria.) They are still around today, for example, as the "scum" on a polluted pond.

Story of a fossil

Fossils are formed mainly from hard parts such as bones, teeth, shells and bark. When an animal or plant dies in water, its remains sink to the sea or river bed, and the soft parts usually rot away. Gradually, sediments such as sand or mud settle on top, burying the remains. Over centuries, the sediments are compressed and cemented together by minerals to form solid rock.

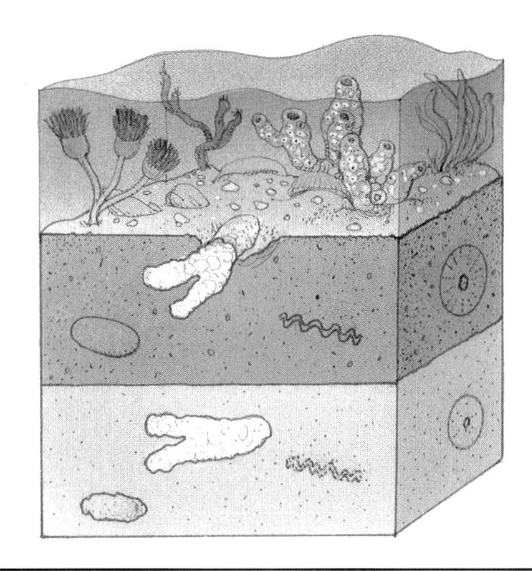

Sponges

The earliest kinds of living things were all one-celled. Sponges are the simplest multi-celled animals. Tiny shards and spikes called spicules make up their internal "skeletons". Their fossils are present in rocks 550 million years old.

Graptolites

These colonial creatures made chains or fans of hard cups that left sawblade-shaped fossils. Scientists are unsure about the actual animals, which may have resembled small worms or anemones. Graptolites died out 300 million years ago.

THE BEGINNING OF LIFE

About 600 million years ago, there was a great evolutionary invention: the shell. In fact, evolution probably came up with this tough, protective casing several times, in different groups of creatures. Until then, animals had been mainly soft-bodied, such as jellyfishes and worms. Within a few tens of millions of years, dozens of new kinds of hard-cased creatures were swimming and crawling in Cambrian seas. The shells have turned out to be a great advantage for us, too. Their toughness meant that they were preserved as fossils much more readily, compared to the exceptionally rare and faint marks left by soft-bodied animals. From the early Cambrian period onwards, the fossil record rapidly becomes much richer and more varied.

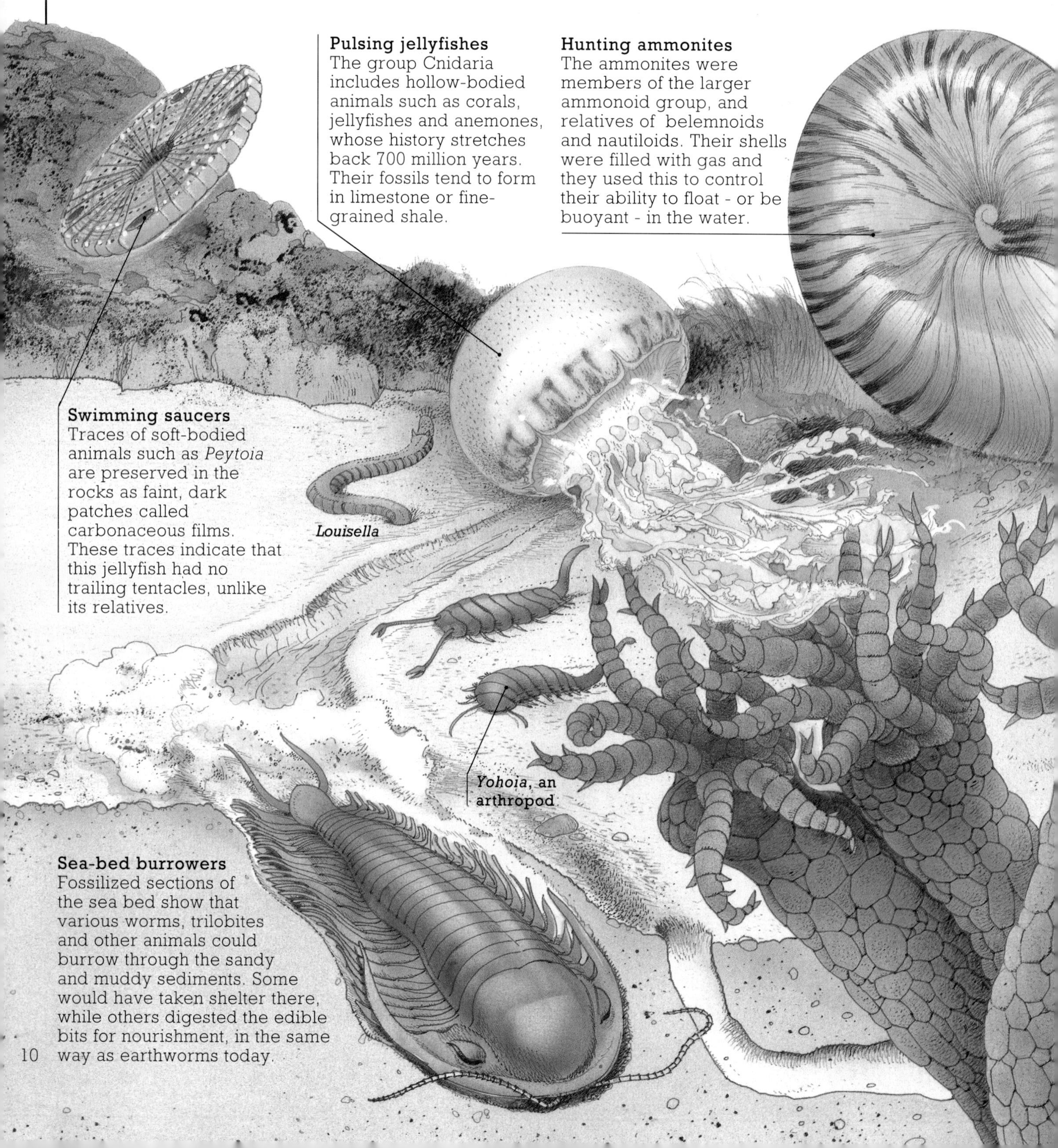

Pulsing jellyfishes
The group Cnidaria includes hollow-bodied animals such as corals, jellyfishes and anemones, whose history stretches back 700 million years. Their fossils tend to form in limestone or fine-grained shale.

Hunting ammonites
The ammonites were members of the larger ammonoid group, and relatives of belemnoids and nautiloids. Their shells were filled with gas and they used this to control their ability to float - or be buoyant - in the water.

Swimming saucers
Traces of soft-bodied animals such as *Peytoia* are preserved in the rocks as faint, dark patches called carbonaceous films. These traces indicate that this jellyfish had no trailing tentacles, unlike its relatives.

Sea-bed burrowers
Fossilized sections of the sea bed show that various worms, trilobites and other animals could burrow through the sandy and muddy sediments. Some would have taken shelter there, while others digested the edible bits for nourishment, in the same way as earthworms today.

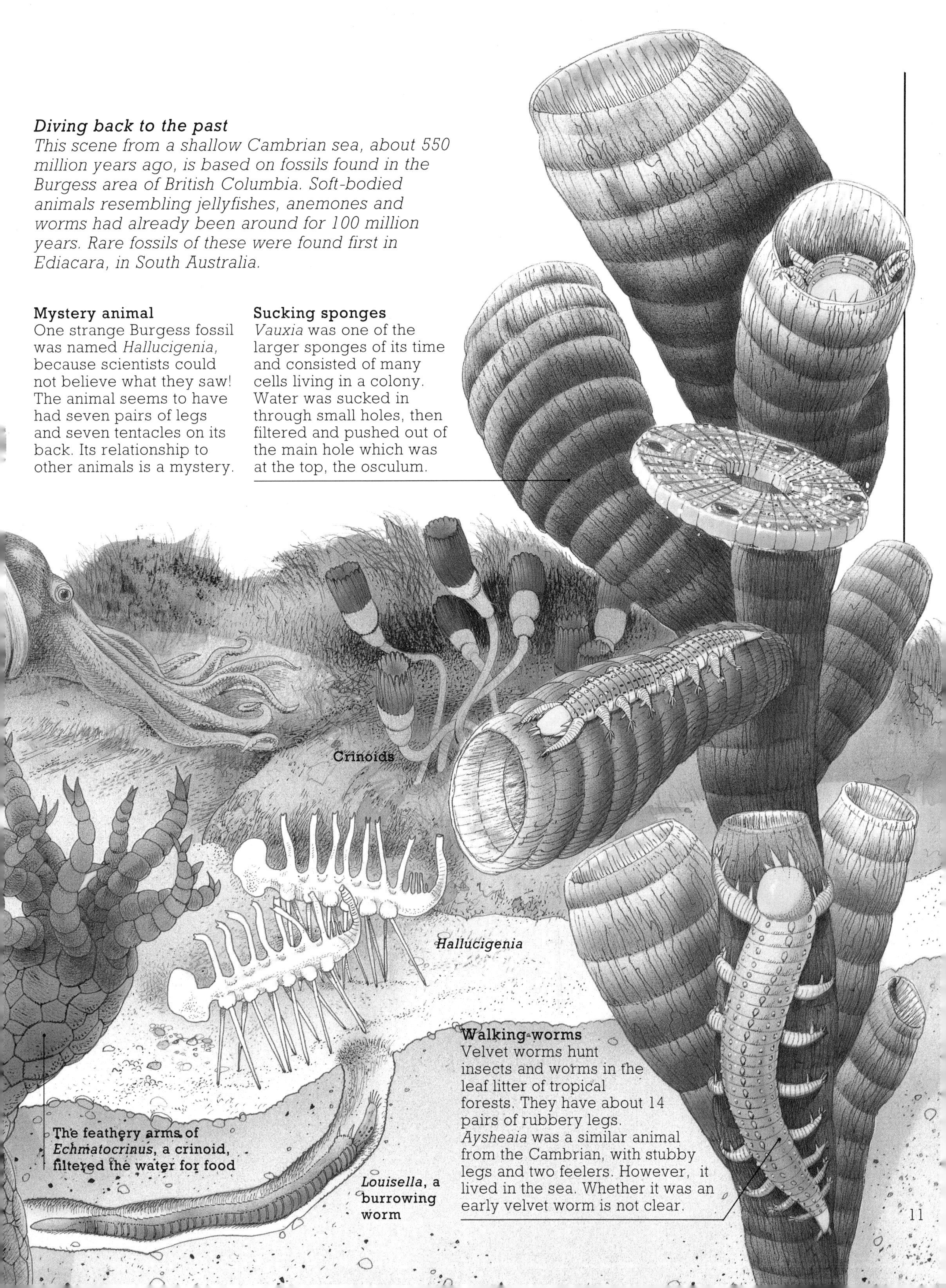

Diving back to the past

This scene from a shallow Cambrian sea, about 550 million years ago, is based on fossils found in the Burgess area of British Columbia. Soft-bodied animals resembling jellyfishes, anemones and worms had already been around for 100 million years. Rare fossils of these were found first in Ediacara, in South Australia.

Mystery animal

One strange Burgess fossil was named *Hallucigenia*, because scientists could not believe what they saw! The animal seems to have had seven pairs of legs and seven tentacles on its back. Its relationship to other animals is a mystery.

Sucking sponges

Vauxia was one of the larger sponges of its time and consisted of many cells living in a colony. Water was sucked in through small holes, then filtered and pushed out of the main hole which was at the top, the osculum.

Walking-worms

Velvet worms hunt insects and worms in the leaf litter of tropical forests. They have about 14 pairs of rubbery legs. *Aysheaia* was a similar animal from the Cambrian, with stubby legs and two feelers. However, it lived in the sea. Whether it was an early velvet worm is not clear.

The feathery arms of *Echmatocrinus*, a crinoid, filtered the water for food

Louisella, **a burrowing worm**

THE CROWDED SEAS

As the Cambrian period passed into that of the Ordovician, living things continued to evolve in the sea. According to the principle of evolution, when animals and plants breed, their offspring are each slightly different. Some offspring are better suited to the conditions at the time, compared to their "sisters and brothers". For example, they might have wider leaves if they are plants, or stronger muscles if they are animals. These offspring have a greater chance of surviving and producing offspring of their own. However, living conditions continue to change. The climate becomes warmer or colder, or a new group of hunting animals appears. So evolution is a continuing process. We see evidence of this particularly in the rich fossil record of the various sea animals of this time.

Legs, arms, tentacles and feelers
Vertebrates are animals with backbones (page 14). The main kinds are fishes, amphibians, reptiles, birds and mammals. About 500 million years ago, there were few vertebrates. The seas belonged to the invertebrates - animals like sponges, jellyfishes, nautiloids and trilobites.

Trilobites
This name means "three-lobed", from the row of three-humped hard plates along the back. The longest trilobites were more than 60cm (2ft), the shortest as small as rice grains. Some had spikes on their shells, and others curled into a ball when in danger.

Sea-scorpions
Also known as eurypterids, these predators had fearsome pincers. They were prehistoric cousins of spiders and scorpions, and their fossils date from about 500 million years ago. The biggest were more than 2.3m (7ft) in length!

Corals
We know today that corals thrive and build their stony reefs in warm waters, with plenty of sunlight. From the extent of their fossils during different prehistoric periods, we can therefore work out how widespread shallow seas were, and the likely climate at the time.

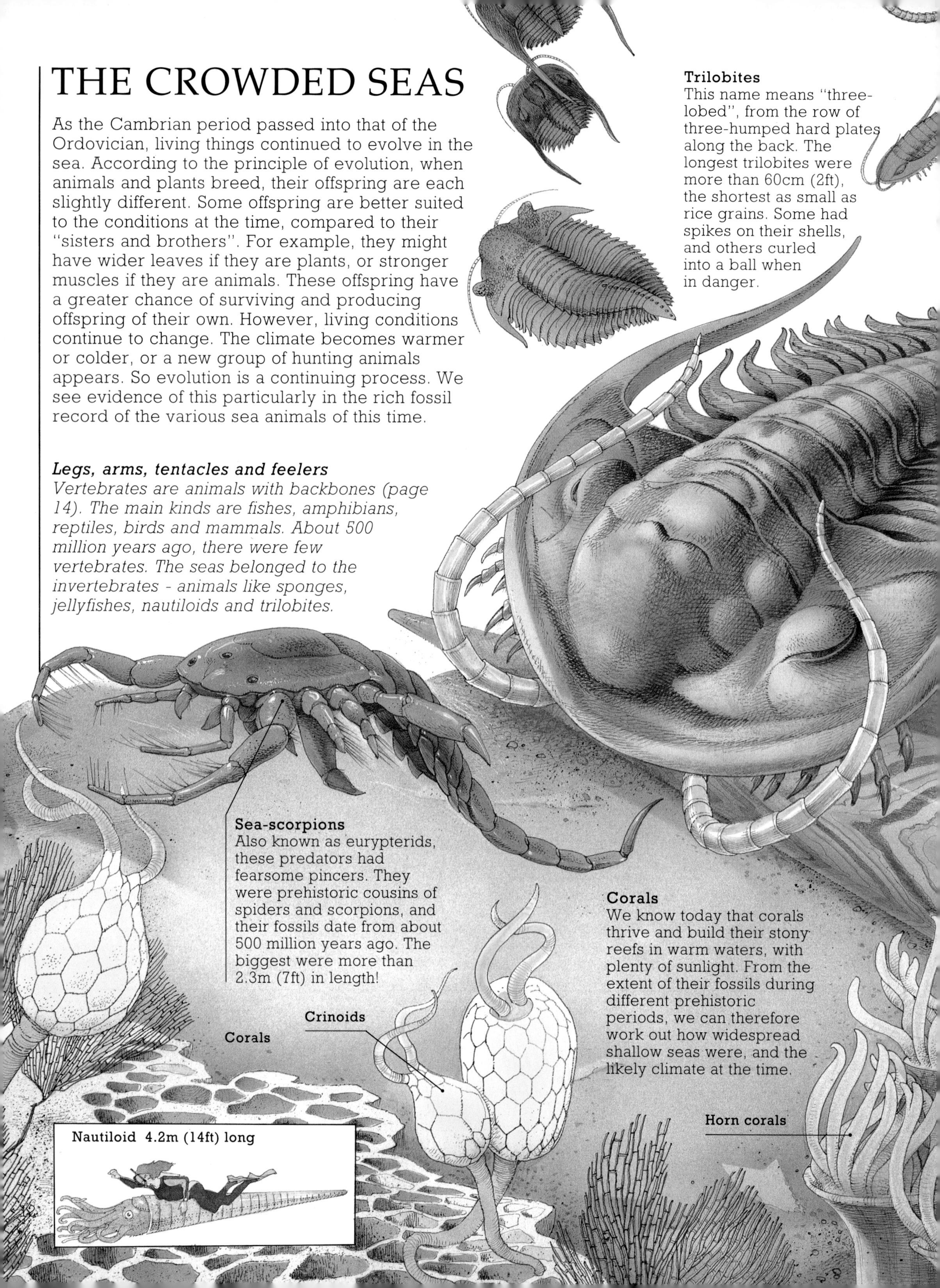

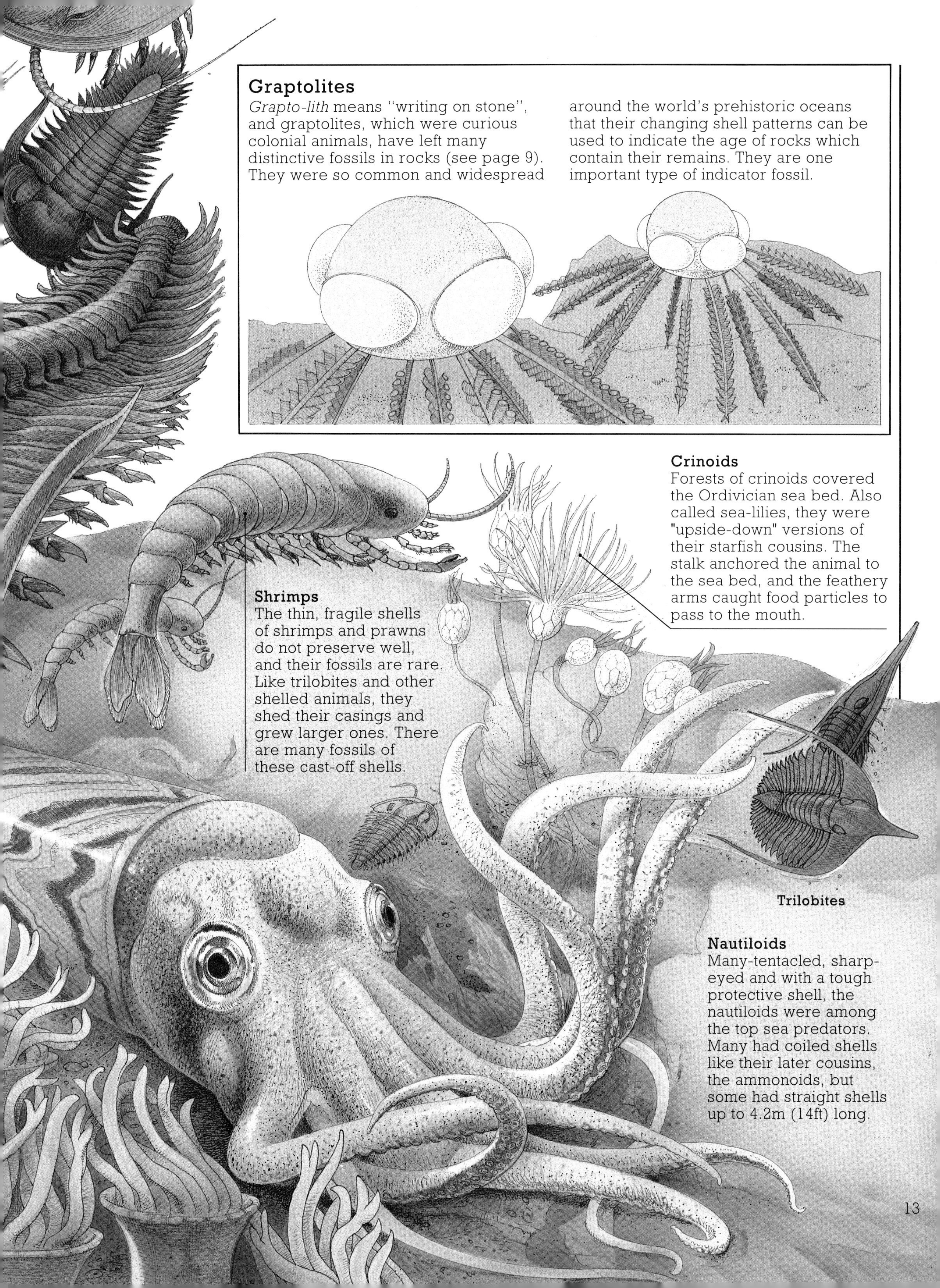

Graptolites

Grapto-lith means "writing on stone", and graptolites, which were curious colonial animals, have left many distinctive fossils in rocks (see page 9). They were so common and widespread around the world's prehistoric oceans that their changing shell patterns can be used to indicate the age of rocks which contain their remains. They are one important type of indicator fossil.

Crinoids

Forests of crinoids covered the Ordovician sea bed. Also called sea-lilies, they were "upside-down" versions of their starfish cousins. The stalk anchored the animal to the sea bed, and the feathery arms caught food particles to pass to the mouth.

Shrimps

The thin, fragile shells of shrimps and prawns do not preserve well, and their fossils are rare. Like trilobites and other shelled animals, they shed their casings and grew larger ones. There are many fossils of these cast-off shells.

Trilobites

Nautiloids

Many-tentacled, sharp-eyed and with a tough protective shell, the nautiloids were among the top sea predators. Many had coiled shells like their later cousins, the ammonoids, but some had straight shells up to 4.2m (14ft) long.

THE AGE OF FISHES

Quite soon (in terms of fossils) after nature had come up with the shell, there was another leap in evolution. By 500 million years ago, the backbone had appeared. This is a flexible row of bones, the vertebrae or spinal column, along the middle of the animal. It provides internal support for the softer parts and anchorage for the strong body-bending muscles. It also protects the main nerves from the brain. Backboned animals are called vertebrates, and the first to evolve were the fishes. The earliest had no fins or jaws; they either sieved water, ate small food particles or rasped at larger lumps. But by about 400 million years ago jaws, too, had been added to the list of evolutionary "inventions".

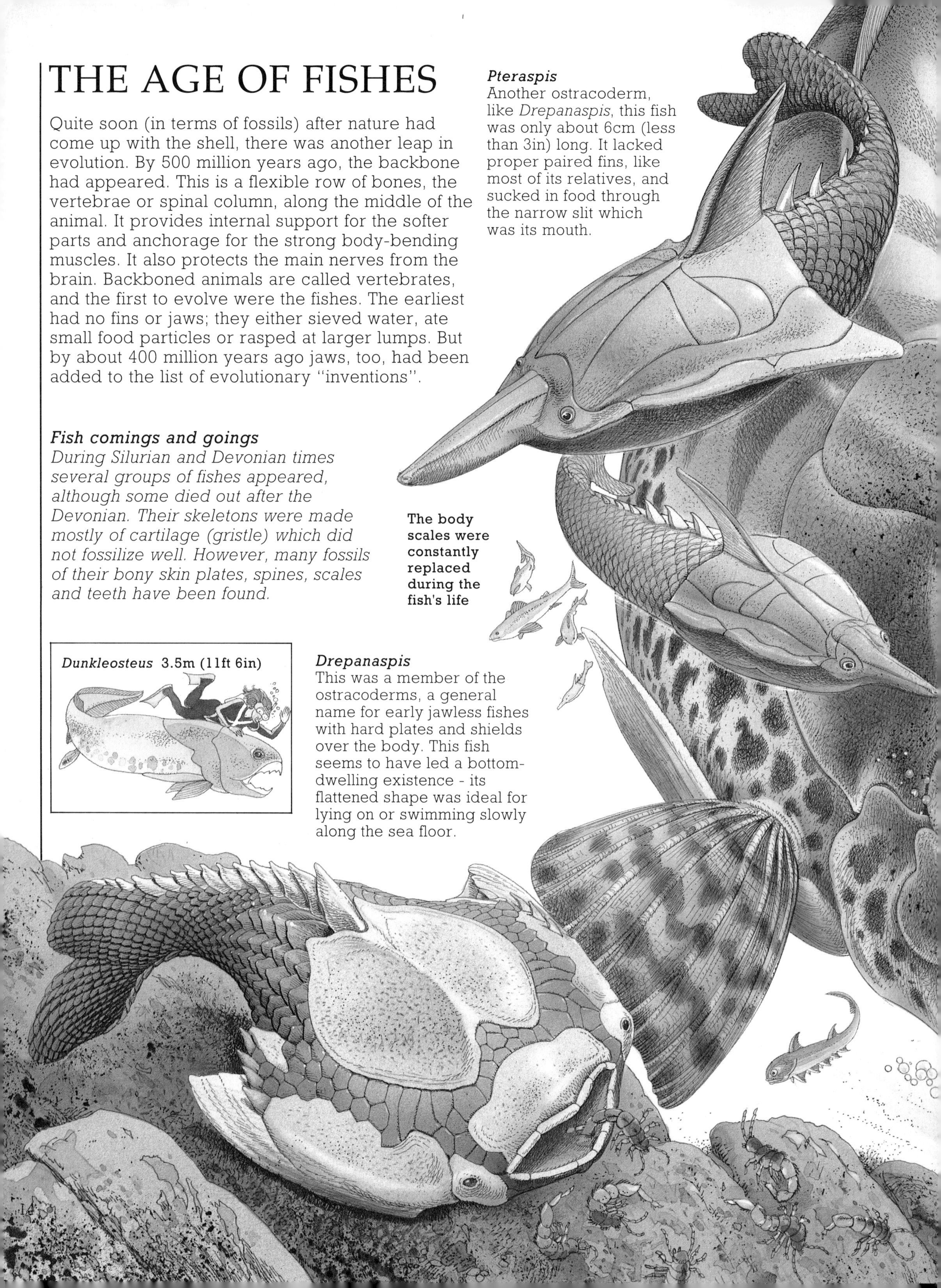

Pteraspis
Another ostracoderm, like *Drepanaspis*, this fish was only about 6cm (less than 3in) long. It lacked proper paired fins, like most of its relatives, and sucked in food through the narrow slit which was its mouth.

Fish comings and goings
During Silurian and Devonian times several groups of fishes appeared, although some died out after the Devonian. Their skeletons were made mostly of cartilage (gristle) which did not fossilize well. However, many fossils of their bony skin plates, spines, scales and teeth have been found.

The body scales were constantly replaced during the fish's life

Dunkleosteus 3.5m (11ft 6in)

Drepanaspis
This was a member of the ostracoderms, a general name for early jawless fishes with hard plates and shields over the body. This fish seems to have led a bottom-dwelling existence - its flattened shape was ideal for lying on or swimming slowly along the sea floor.

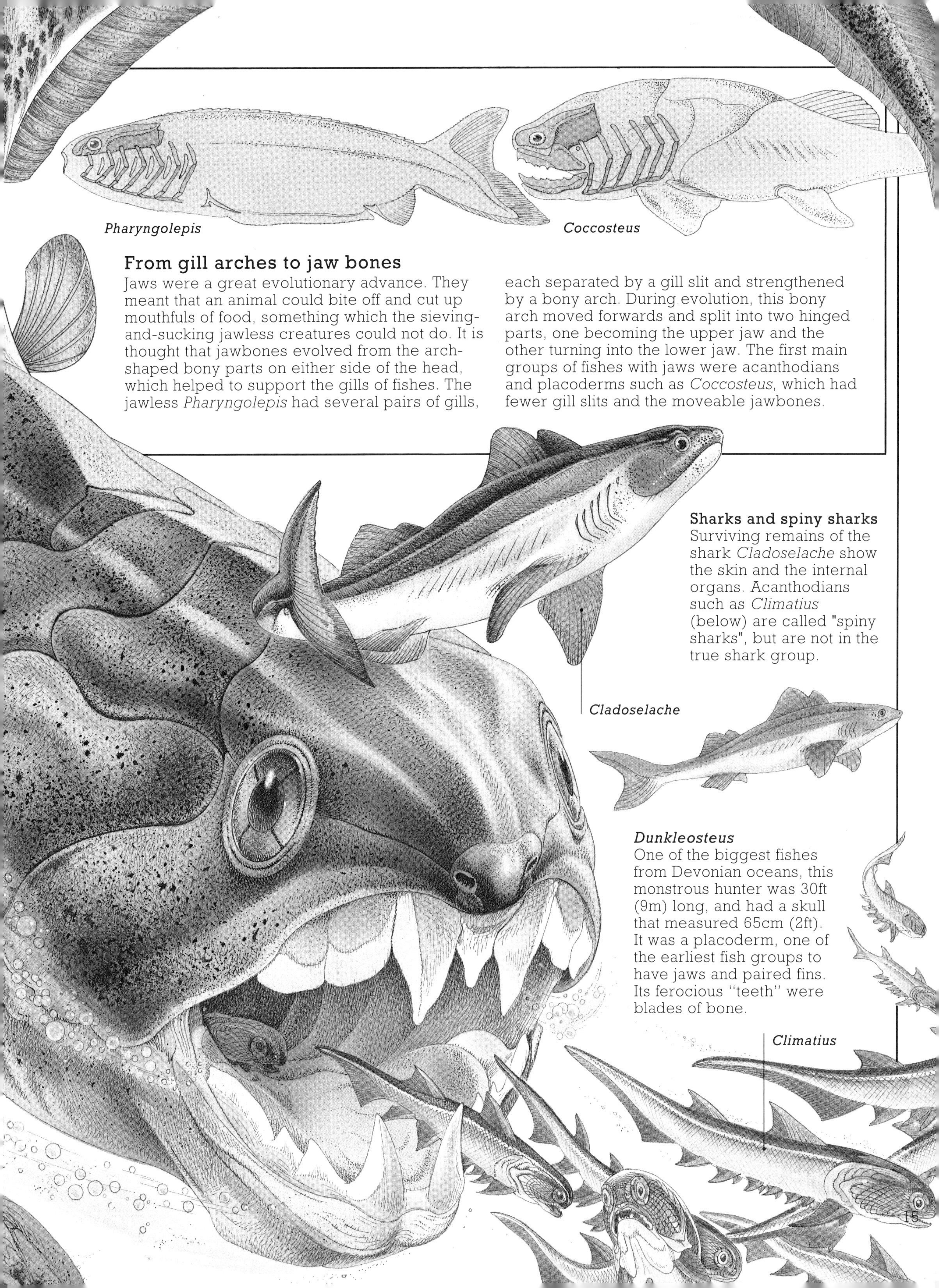

From gill arches to jaw bones

Jaws were a great evolutionary advance. They meant that an animal could bite off and cut up mouthfuls of food, something which the sieving-and-sucking jawless creatures could not do. It is thought that jawbones evolved from the arch-shaped bony parts on either side of the head, which helped to support the gills of fishes. The jawless *Pharyngolepis* had several pairs of gills, each separated by a gill slit and strengthened by a bony arch. During evolution, this bony arch moved forwards and split into two hinged parts, one becoming the upper jaw and the other turning into the lower jaw. The first main groups of fishes with jaws were acanthodians and placoderms such as *Coccosteus*, which had fewer gill slits and the moveable jawbones.

Sharks and spiny sharks
Surviving remains of the shark *Cladoselache* show the skin and the internal organs. Acanthodians such as *Climatius* (below) are called "spiny sharks", but are not in the true shark group.

Dunkleosteus
One of the biggest fishes from Devonian oceans, this monstrous hunter was 30ft (9m) long, and had a skull that measured 65cm (2ft). It was a placoderm, one of the earliest fish groups to have jaws and paired fins. Its ferocious "teeth" were blades of bone.

A PLACE TO LIVE

For hundreds of millions of years, Earth's landscape was rocky and barren. While plants and animals thrived in the sea, the land was bare. This was probably because, at first, the mixture of gases which made up the atmosphere was poisonous to living things. In particular, there was a lack of oxygen, the gas that plants and animals need to "breathe" in order to stay alive. Also, the atmosphere did not screen the Sun's rays as it does today, so that damaging radiation reached the surface. In water, plants and animals were protected. However, the activities of blue-green algae in surface waters produced oxygen, by the light-trapping process of photosynthesis. This caused oxygen and radiation-filtering gases to build up slowly in the atmosphere. At last the gas mixture and radiation level were suitable for life, and the invasion of the land began.

The prehistoric mini-jungle
It is likely that plants were the first living things on land. The oldest fossils of land plants date from more than 400 million years ago. By the Devonian period, several types of plants had evolved, along with animals which ate them - and predators which hunted them.

Herbivores
As soon as plants gained a hold on land, animals followed to eat them. With few competitors, many creatures began to evolve. Millipedes, worms and primitive insects such as cockroaches were among these dry-land pioneers. As animals and plants died and rotted, the first patches of soil formed on the bare rock.

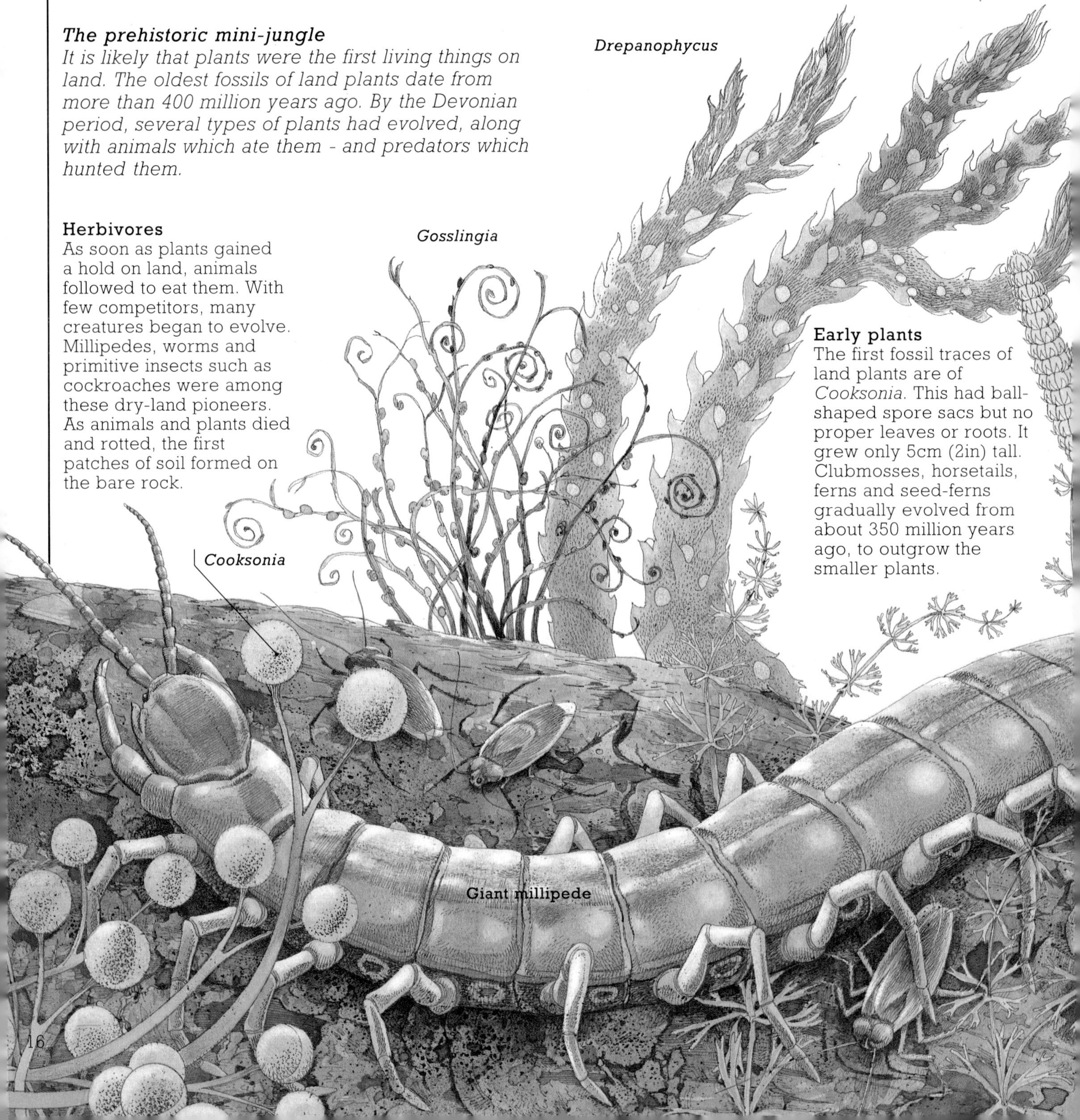

Early plants
The first fossil traces of land plants are of *Cooksonia*. This had ball-shaped spore sacs but no proper leaves or roots. It grew only 5cm (2in) tall. Clubmosses, horsetails, ferns and seed-ferns gradually evolved from about 350 million years ago, to outgrow the smaller plants.

Carnivores

The herbivorous land animals represented a new source of food, and it was not long before land carnivores appeared to prey on them. By 370 million years ago, spiders were hunting their victims among the plant stems.

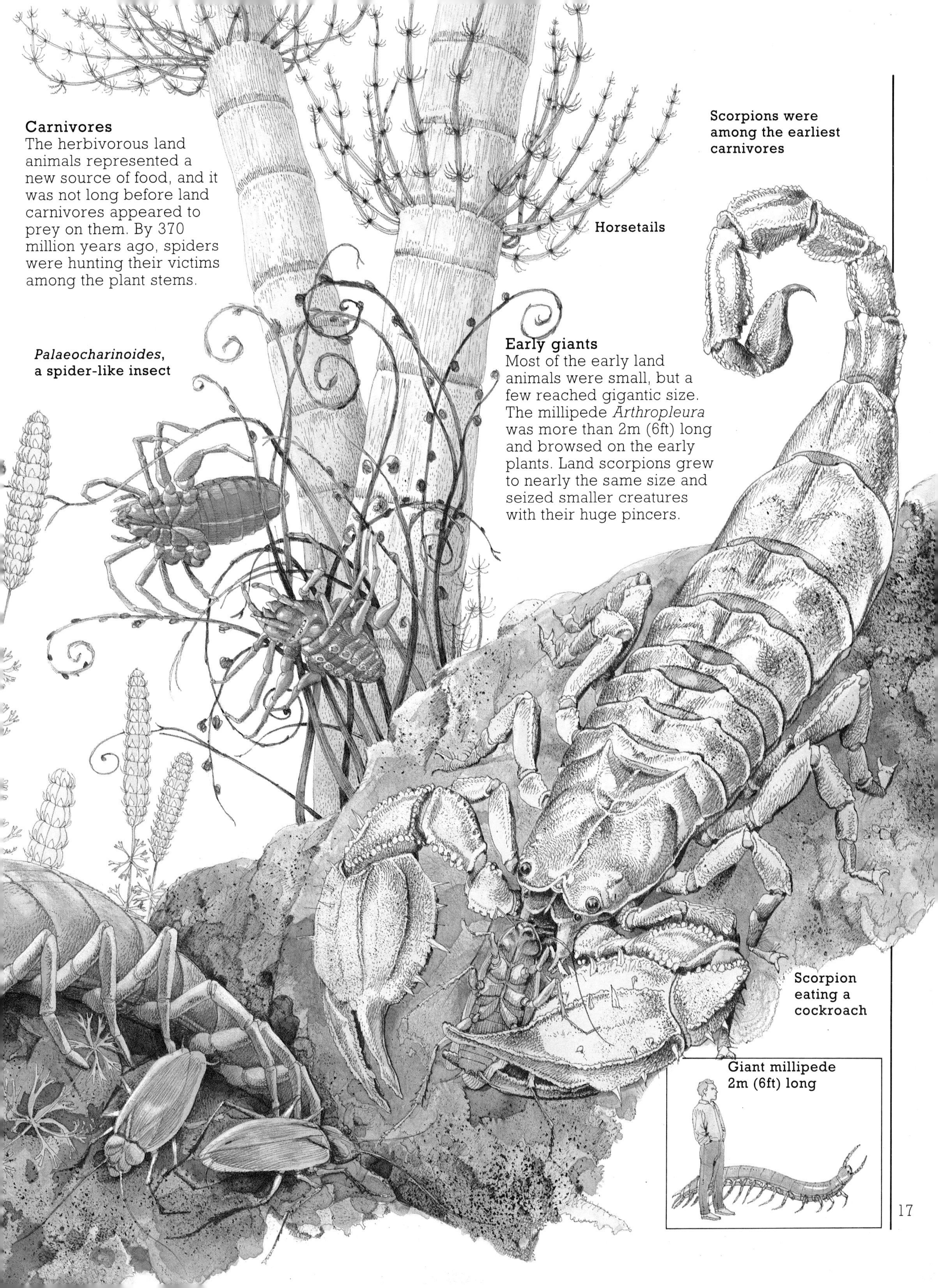

Early giants

Most of the early land animals were small, but a few reached gigantic size. The millipede *Arthropleura* was more than 2m (6ft) long and browsed on the early plants. Land scorpions grew to nearly the same size and seized smaller creatures with their huge pincers.

FISH OUT OF WATER

At the same time as the land was being colonized by plants and invertebrate animals (those with no backbones), the first vertebrates were gaining a foothold. The foot probably developed from the fin in a group of fishes called rhipidistians, about 370 million years ago. Along with the evolution of limbs and feet came the ability to breathe air. If an ancient lake dried up, any fishes which could struggle overland to another pool, gulping in air along the way, would be able to survive and breed offspring with that ability. So these fishes evolved into the first land vertebrates - the amphibians.

The Age of Amphibians

300 million years ago, amphibians dominated the swampy countryside. This array shows how the group became more independent of the water, with more waterproof bodies and stronger legs. However they never completely broke away. They had to return to water to lay their eggs, as amphibians do today.

Ichthyostega

Near the end of the Devonian period, this 1m (3ft) long beast lumbered from water to land. It is the oldest known tetrapod, or four-limbed animal. It still possessed fish-like scales and a fishy tail, but it walked on four five-toed feet. Probably its skin was not very watertight, so it stayed in or near freshwater rivers and lakes, hunting along the shores for fish.

Frogs and salamanders

Along with toads, newts and the worm-shaped caecilians, frogs and salamanders are the living amphibians. *Karaurus*, which was about 20cm (8in) in length, was one of the first salamanders. Even so, it did not appear until 150 million years ago. *Triadobatrachus* is one of the first frogs, known from fossils 220 million years old found on Madagascar.

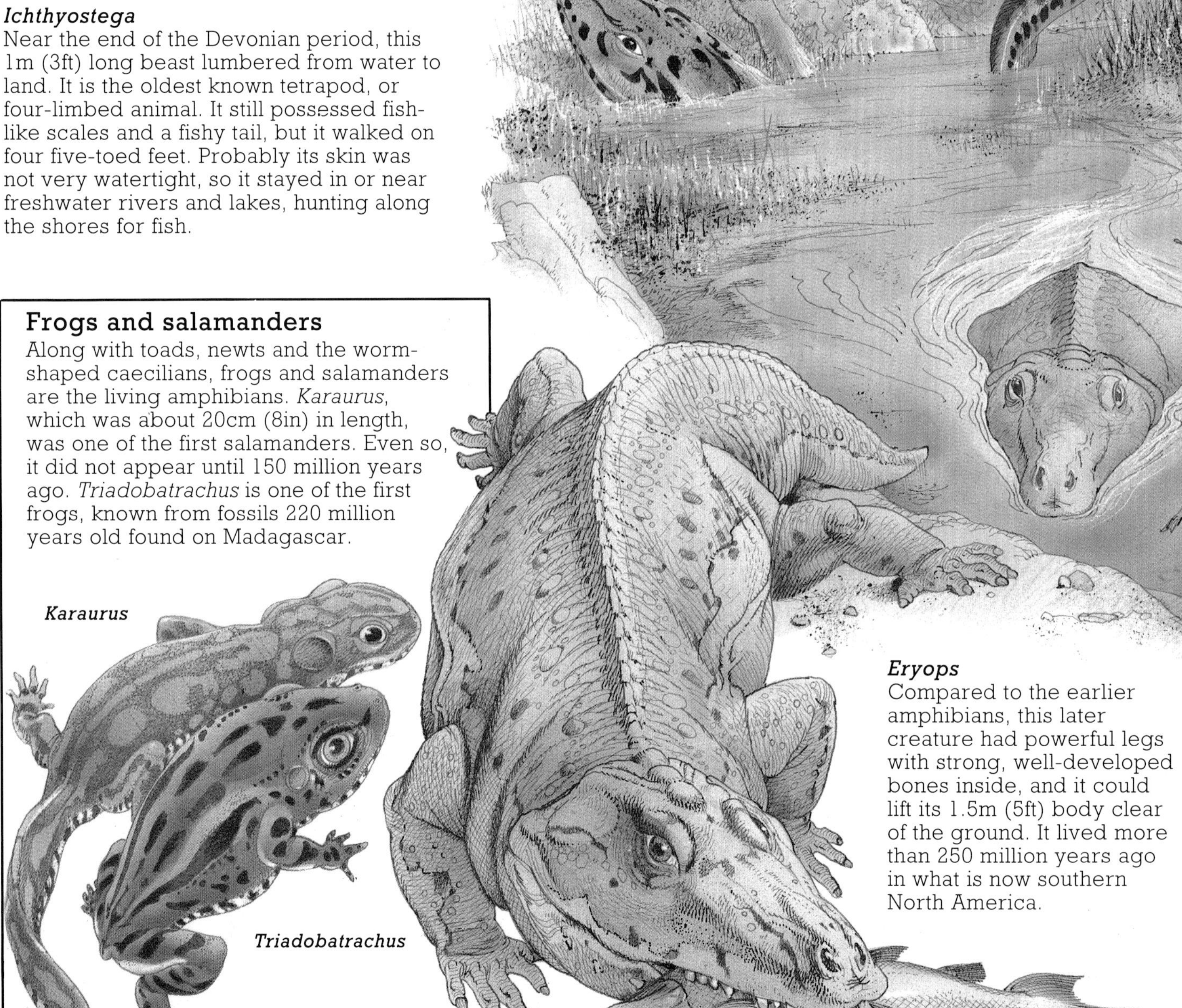

Eryops

Compared to the earlier amphibians, this later creature had powerful legs with strong, well-developed bones inside, and it could lift its 1.5m (5ft) body clear of the ground. It lived more than 250 million years ago in what is now southern North America.

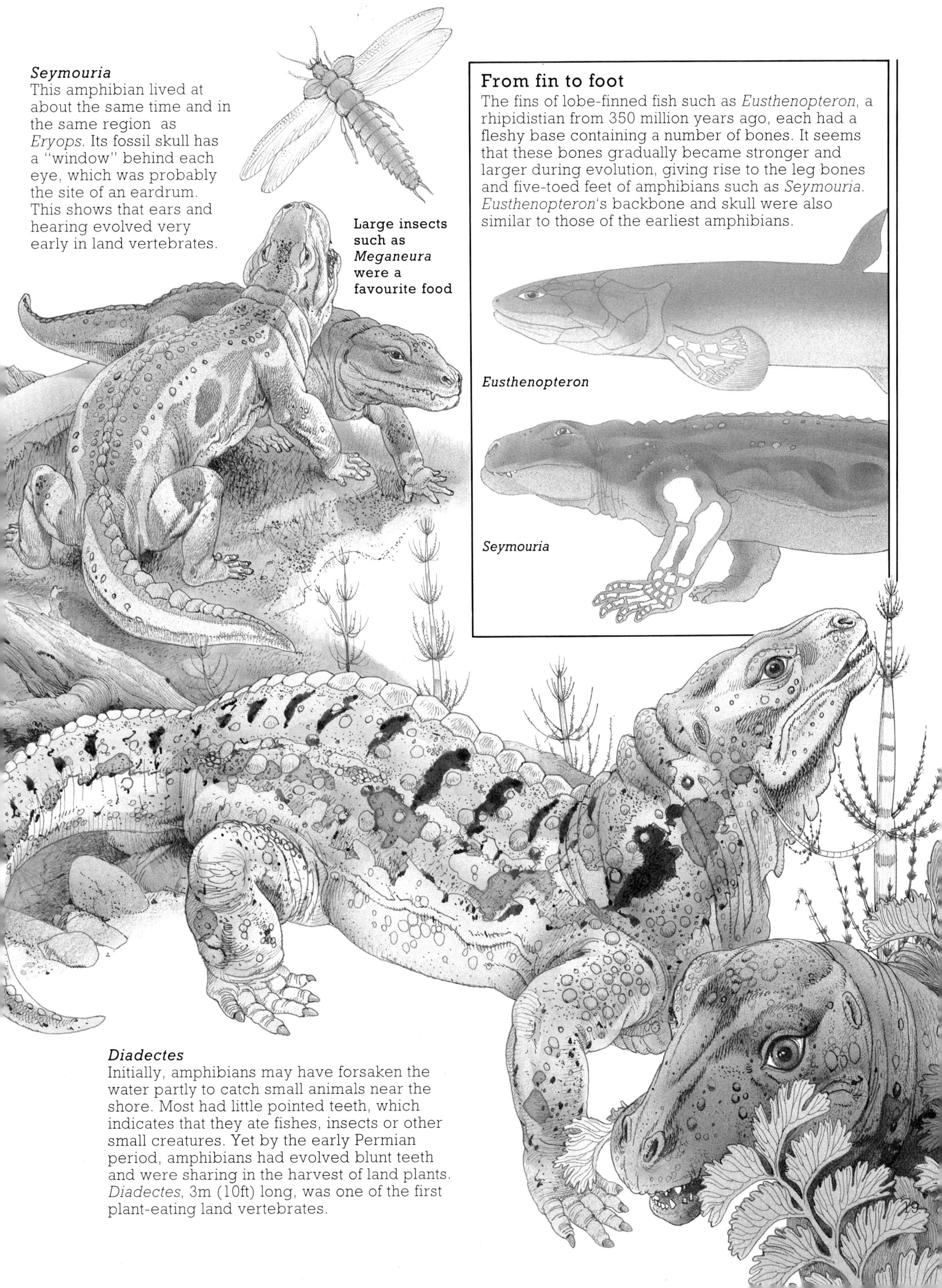

Seymouria
This amphibian lived at about the same time and in the same region as *Eryops*. Its fossil skull has a "window" behind each eye, which was probably the site of an eardrum. This shows that ears and hearing evolved very early in land vertebrates.

Large insects such as *Meganeura* were a favourite food

From fin to foot

The fins of lobe-finned fish such as *Eusthenopteron*, a rhipidistian from 350 million years ago, each had a fleshy base containing a number of bones. It seems that these bones gradually became stronger and larger during evolution, giving rise to the leg bones and five-toed feet of amphibians such as *Seymouria*. *Eusthenopteron*'s backbone and skull were also similar to those of the earliest amphibians.

Eusthenopteron

Seymouria

Diadectes
Initially, amphibians may have forsaken the water partly to catch small animals near the shore. Most had little pointed teeth, which indicates that they ate fishes, insects or other small creatures. Yet by the early Permian period, amphibians had evolved blunt teeth and were sharing in the harvest of land plants. *Diadectes*, 3m (10ft) long, was one of the first plant-eating land vertebrates.

EARLY REPTILES

Dinosaurs may be the most famous prehistoric reptiles, but they were far from being the only ones. In fact the reptiles were an enormous and varied group, which first appeared in numbers about 300 million years ago. Some 50 million years later they had risen to dominate the land. Formerly, one of the earliest reptiles was thought to be *Hylonomus* from late Carboniferous times. But recent fossil discoveries in Scotland, of a lizard-like creature nicknamed "Lizzie", have pushed back their history even further, to 350 million years ago. It would appear that amphibians had only just developed when the reptiles evolved from one or more amphibian groups. The reptiles' great evolutionary "inventions" were hard scales and the shelled egg (page 29). No longer did they have to stay near water to moisten their skin and breed - they could roam far inland.

Prehistoric combine-harvester
About 250 million years ago, the huge plant-eater Moschops *munched its way through the vegetation of what we now call southern Africa. It was a member of the therapsid group of mammal-like reptiles, and lived about the same time as its mammal-like-reptile relative* Dimetrodon *(page 22).*

Body and neck
Moschops was one of the biggest animals of its age, with an appetite to match. Fossils of *Moschops*' skull, and its sturdy neck and shoulder bones, reveal areas for the anchorage of powerful muscles.

Head
Moschops had very thick bone on the top of its skull. It may have held head-butting contests with rivals, in order to win mating partners, like rams do today (pages 40-41).

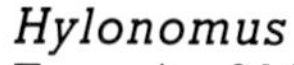

Hylonomus
From its 310 million-year-old fossils, this long-tailed reptile can be reconstructed as a long-legged, actively-moving land predator. It looked like a lizard but in fact belonged to a different group, the cotylosaurs or "stem reptiles".

***Moschops*' teeth were chisel-shaped for cutting off plant parts**

Plants
Rocks from the Permian period show that there were dry conditions in many places. Plants adapted as their soft, lush leaves became tougher and stringier. Animals had to evolve with them and develop stronger-chewing teeth and jaws.

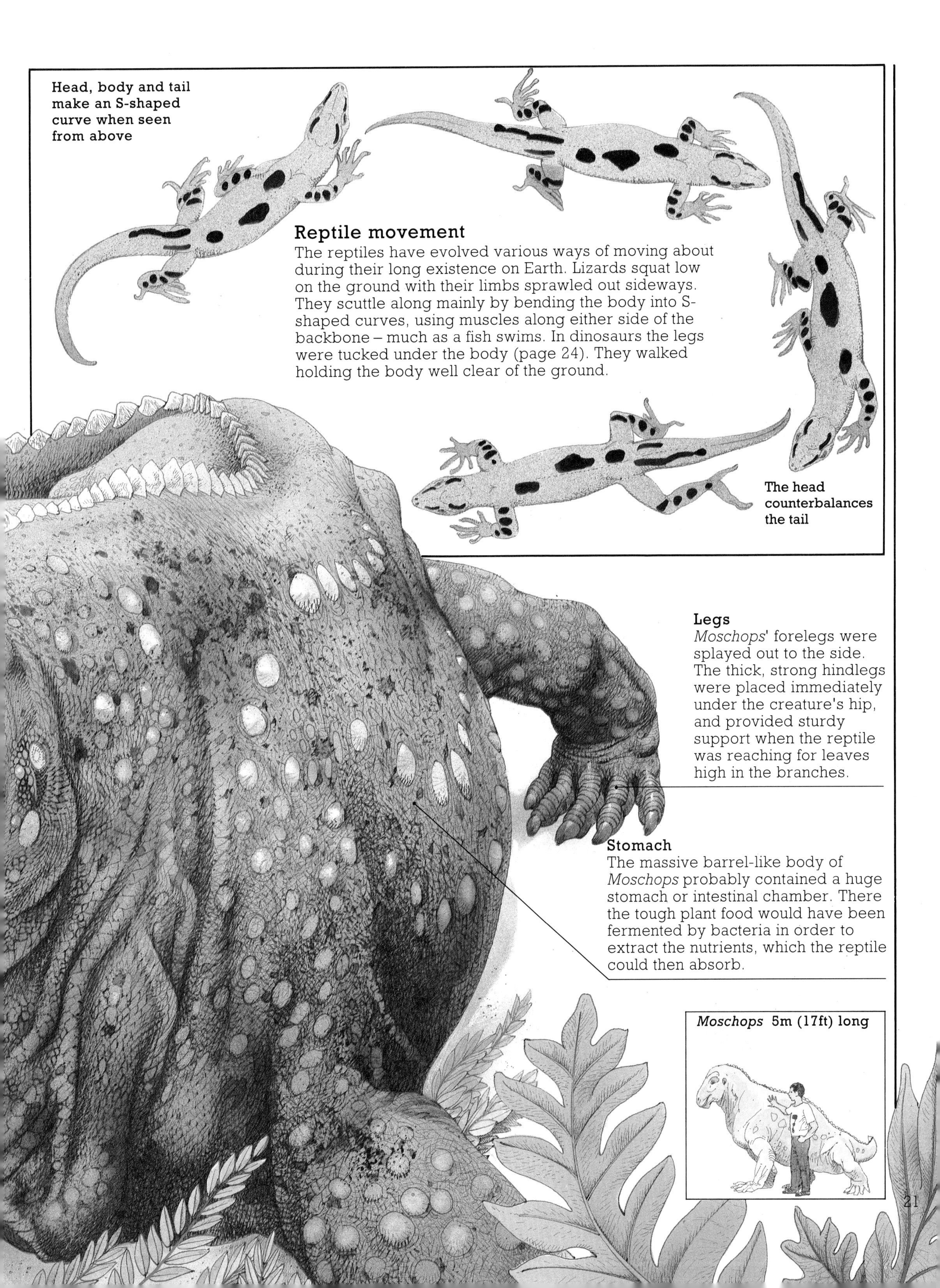

Reptile movement

The reptiles have evolved various ways of moving about during their long existence on Earth. Lizards squat low on the ground with their limbs sprawled out sideways. They scuttle along mainly by bending the body into S-shaped curves, using muscles along either side of the backbone – much as a fish swims. In dinosaurs the legs were tucked under the body (page 24). They walked holding the body well clear of the ground.

Legs
Moschops' forelegs were splayed out to the side. The thick, strong hindlegs were placed immediately under the creature's hip, and provided sturdy support when the reptile was reaching for leaves high in the branches.

Stomach
The massive barrel-like body of *Moschops* probably contained a huge stomach or intestinal chamber. There the tough plant food would have been fermented by bacteria in order to extract the nutrients, which the reptile could then absorb.

Moschops 5m (17ft) long

TALE OF THE SAIL

By 200 million years ago, several large groups of reptiles had already evolved, enjoyed a spell of success, and then disappeared. Among them were the mammal-like reptiles. They are so-named because their fossil skeletons have many features in common with mammals - indeed, mammals evolved from them. There were two main types. One was the pelycosaurs such as *Dimetrodon*, which dominated many regions around 280-250 million years ago. The others were therapsids like *Moschops* (page 20-21), who took over from the pelycosaurs, but were overshadowed 50 million years later by the dinosaurs.

Rhynchosaurs
During the Triassic period the rhynchosaurs or "beak-heads", such as *Hyperodapedon*, were very successful for a short period. Their curious jaws and teeth were probably adapted for holding, chopping and crushing leathery plants.

Hyperodapedon

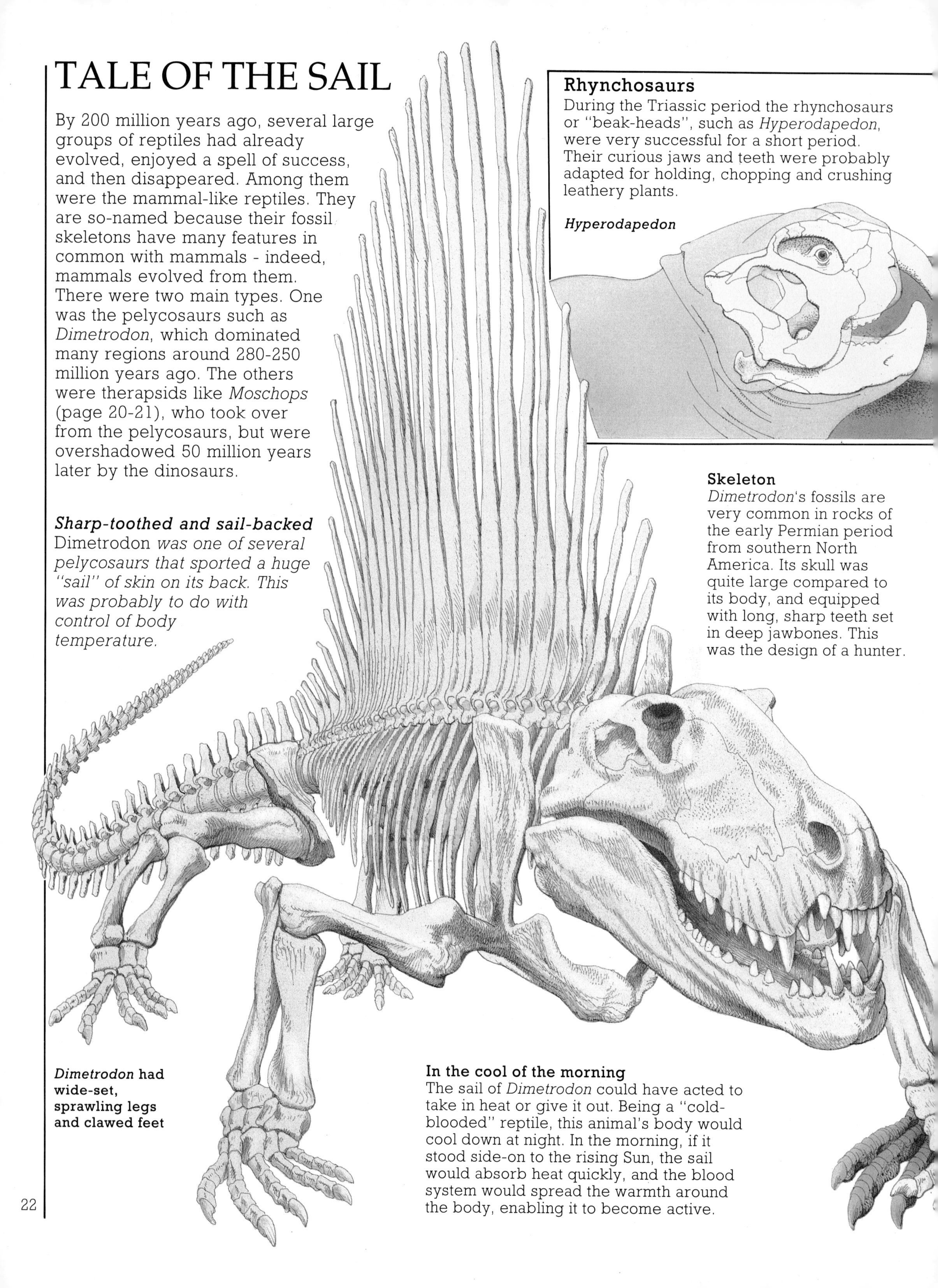

Sharp-toothed and sail-backed
Dimetrodon *was one of several pelycosaurs that sported a huge "sail" of skin on its back. This was probably to do with control of body temperature.*

Skeleton
Dimetrodon's fossils are very common in rocks of the early Permian period from southern North America. Its skull was quite large compared to its body, and equipped with long, sharp teeth set in deep jawbones. This was the design of a hunter.

***Dimetrodon* had wide-set, sprawling legs and clawed feet**

In the cool of the morning
The sail of *Dimetrodon* could have acted to take in heat or give it out. Being a "cold-blooded" reptile, this animal's body would cool down at night. In the morning, if it stood side-on to the rising Sun, the sail would absorb heat quickly, and the blood system would spread the warmth around the body, enabling it to become active.

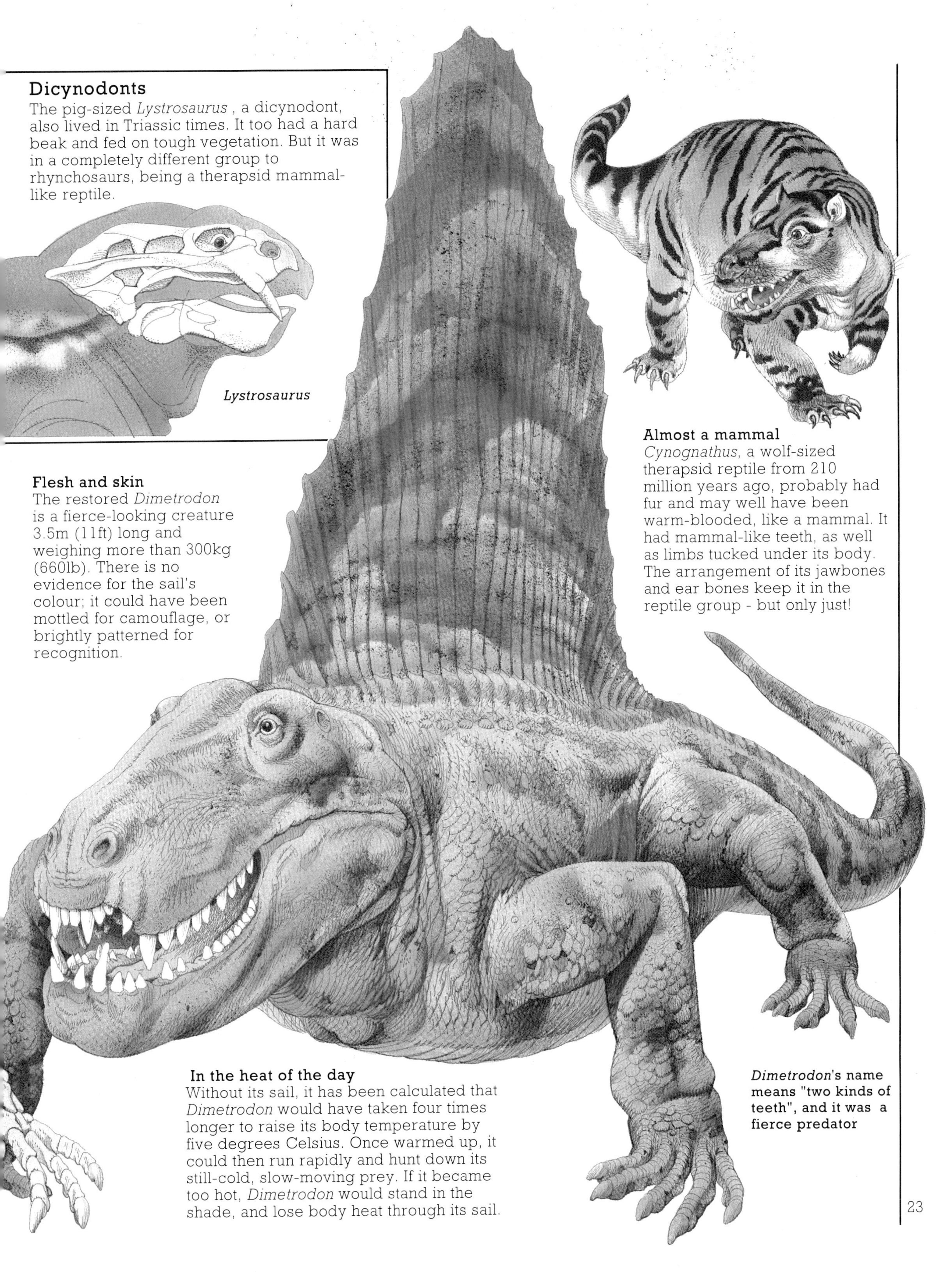

Dicynodonts

The pig-sized *Lystrosaurus* , a dicynodont, also lived in Triassic times. It too had a hard beak and fed on tough vegetation. But it was in a completely different group to rhynchosaurs, being a therapsid mammal-like reptile.

Lystrosaurus

Almost a mammal
Cynognathus, a wolf-sized therapsid reptile from 210 million years ago, probably had fur and may well have been warm-blooded, like a mammal. It had mammal-like teeth, as well as limbs tucked under its body. The arrangement of its jawbones and ear bones keep it in the reptile group - but only just!

Flesh and skin
The restored *Dimetrodon* is a fierce-looking creature 3.5m (11ft) long and weighing more than 300kg (660lb). There is no evidence for the sail's colour; it could have been mottled for camouflage, or brightly patterned for recognition.

In the heat of the day
Without its sail, it has been calculated that *Dimetrodon* would have taken four times longer to raise its body temperature by five degrees Celsius. Once warmed up, it could then run rapidly and hunt down its still-cold, slow-moving prey. If it became too hot, *Dimetrodon* would stand in the shade, and lose body heat through its sail.

***Dimetrodon*'s name means "two kinds of teeth", and it was a fierce predator**

ENTER THE DINOSAURS!

From about 215 million years ago, for more than 150 million years, the group of reptiles known as dinosaurs ruled the world. Or, to be more accurate, they ruled the land. There were no swimming or flying dinosaurs. Other groups of reptiles soared in the air and splashed through the seas (pages 32 and 38). The dinosaurs evolved into an amazing variety of shapes and sizes, including swift, two-footed predators and lumbering, four-legged, armoured plant-eaters. One reason for their great success was probably their limb design. A dinosaur's legs were tucked under the body, so that it could walk upright on them, rather than being splayed out at the side like a crocodile or lizard (page 21). This helped dinosaurs to move quickly and without wasting too much energy.

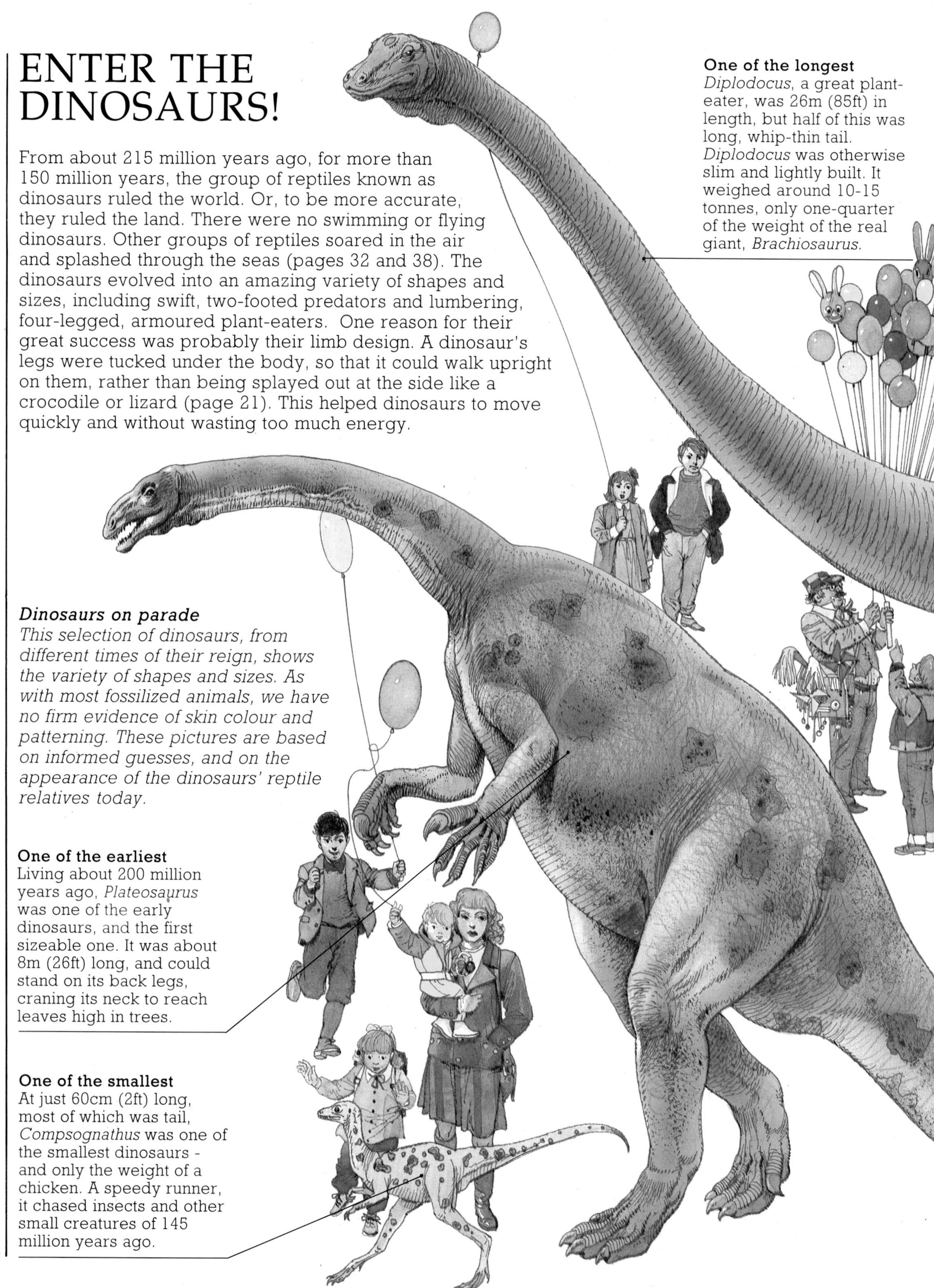

One of the longest
Diplodocus, a great plant-eater, was 26m (85ft) in length, but half of this was long, whip-thin tail. *Diplodocus* was otherwise slim and lightly built. It weighed around 10-15 tonnes, only one-quarter of the weight of the real giant, *Brachiosaurus*.

Dinosaurs on parade
This selection of dinosaurs, from different times of their reign, shows the variety of shapes and sizes. As with most fossilized animals, we have no firm evidence of skin colour and patterning. These pictures are based on informed guesses, and on the appearance of the dinosaurs' reptile relatives today.

One of the earliest
Living about 200 million years ago, *Plateosaurus* was one of the early dinosaurs, and the first sizeable one. It was about 8m (26ft) long, and could stand on its back legs, craning its neck to reach leaves high in trees.

One of the smallest
At just 60cm (2ft) long, most of which was tail, *Compsognathus* was one of the smallest dinosaurs - and only the weight of a chicken. A speedy runner, it chased insects and other small creatures of 145 million years ago.

One of the fiercest
About 140 million years ago, the great meat-eating *Allosaurus* strode across what is known now as North America. It was 12m (39ft) long and had fearsome stabbing teeth as big as an adult human's hand. It used its strong claws to hold down and tear at its prey.

One of the fleetest
At 4m (13ft), *Gallimimus* was one of the largest "ostrich dinosaurs". Its 70-million-year-old fossils were found in Mongolia. With large eyes and long, ostrich-type legs, it could spot and run down smaller prey such as lizards and flying insects.

One of the commonest
Iguanodon is one of the best-known dinosaurs. Many fossils have been found, often in groups (page 28). It lived some 120 million years ago. The large thumb spikes may have been used to fend off predators or pull branches to its mouth.

The secret in the hips

The dinosaurs on these two pages were from the ornithischian or "bird-hipped" group, as explained on the right. (Those on the previous two pages were saurischian or "lizard-hipped".) These were average- to large-sized plant-eaters, often with duck-like beaked mouths, and horns, frills, tubes or crests on their heads.

One of the dumbest?
A small relative of the famous *Stegosaurus*, the 2.5m (8ft) *Kentrosaurus* from Africa also had a very small brain for its body size. Yet brain-power could not have been everything, for stegosaurid dinosaurs were common for more than 70 million years.

One of the last
Triceratops, named for its three face horns, lived about 70-64 million years ago, at the end of the Age of Dinosaurs. It was 9m (30ft) long and 5 tonnes in weight. The horns and bony neck frill would have given good protection against predators of the time, such as *Tyrannosaurus* (page 31).

Bird or lizard hips?

Dinosaurs fall into two main groups, depending on the shape of the bones in the hips. The "lizard-hipped" types had one bone, the pubis, sticking forwards and downwards, like lizards have today. In the "bird-hipped" types, this bone pointed backwards, parallel with the hip bones, as in birds. Such clues, revealed by fossil bones, are useful for studying how dinosaurs evolved and how the groups are related.

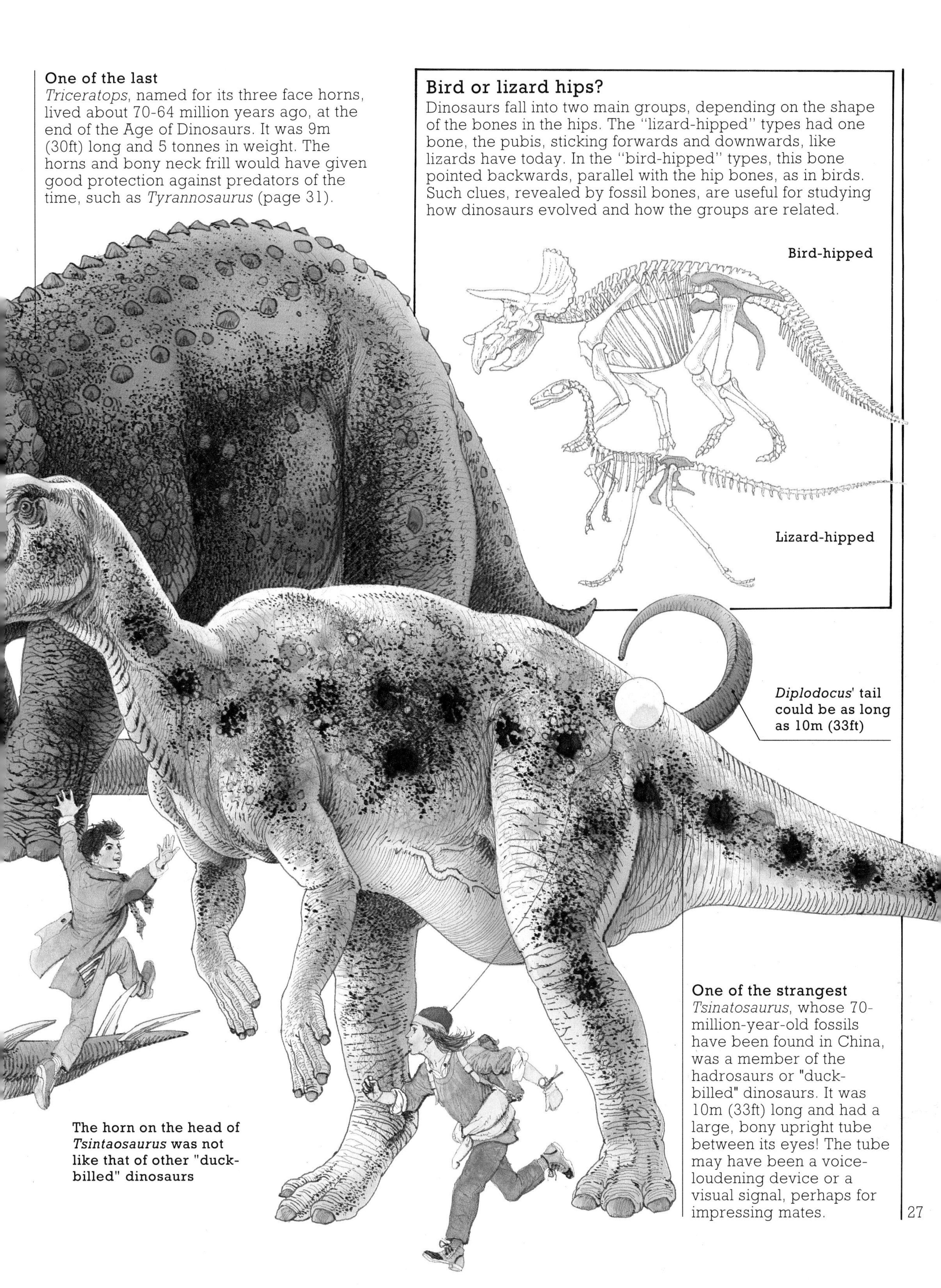

***Diplodocus*' tail could be as long as 10m (33ft)**

The horn on the head of *Tsintaosaurus* was not like that of other "duck-billed" dinosaurs

One of the strangest
Tsinatosaurus, whose 70-million-year-old fossils have been found in China, was a member of the hadrosaurs or "duck-billed" dinosaurs. It was 10m (33ft) long and had a large, bony upright tube between its eyes! The tube may have been a voice-loudening device or a visual signal, perhaps for impressing mates.

GENTLE GIANTS

From about 1978, groups of fossilized dinosaur nests, eggs, newly-hatched babies and young have been found in Montana, USA. They were of *Maiasaura*, a duck-billed dinosaur (pages 26-27). Some of the smaller individuals were only 1m (3ft) long. Some had worn teeth, indicating that they had eaten plant food. Either they had gone to find the food and then come back to the nest, or other dinosaurs had brought it to them. The overall picture is of a dinosaur nesting colony where parents guarded their eggs, babies and young, and probably brought them food. Perhaps a disaster struck and the parents were forced to run away, but the strong homing instinct of the young made them stay near the nests - where they were overwhelmed. Further fossil evidence is now showing us about dinosaur family life, and that many kinds of dinosaur lived, travelled and bred in groups.

Journey across America
About 75 million years ago, this could have been the scene in western North America. Corythosaurus *was a duck-billed dinosaur, well known from numerous fossil bones discovered there. Several skeletons preserved in the same small area point to group travel. This would give safety in numbers from lurking predators.*

Crest and nose
The bony crest of *Corythosaurus* looked like a fan stuck onto its head! The crest was about 30cm (1ft) tall, mostly hollow and contained long, curved air passages from the inner nasal cavity. These twisted around and went back to the nostrils on the snout.

Beak and teeth
The hard, biting "beak" at the front of the mouth could pull and snip off food. Towards the back of the mouth were hundreds of cheek teeth in rows, with ridged surfaces, ideal for grinding tough food.

Stomach and food
One fossil specimen of *Corythosaurus* had pine needles and twigs preserved in its stomach area, so it is presumed that this was at least part of its diet. It may also have browsed on magnolias and other flowering plants (pages 40-41).

Corythosaurus **would have been able to run away from predators on two legs**

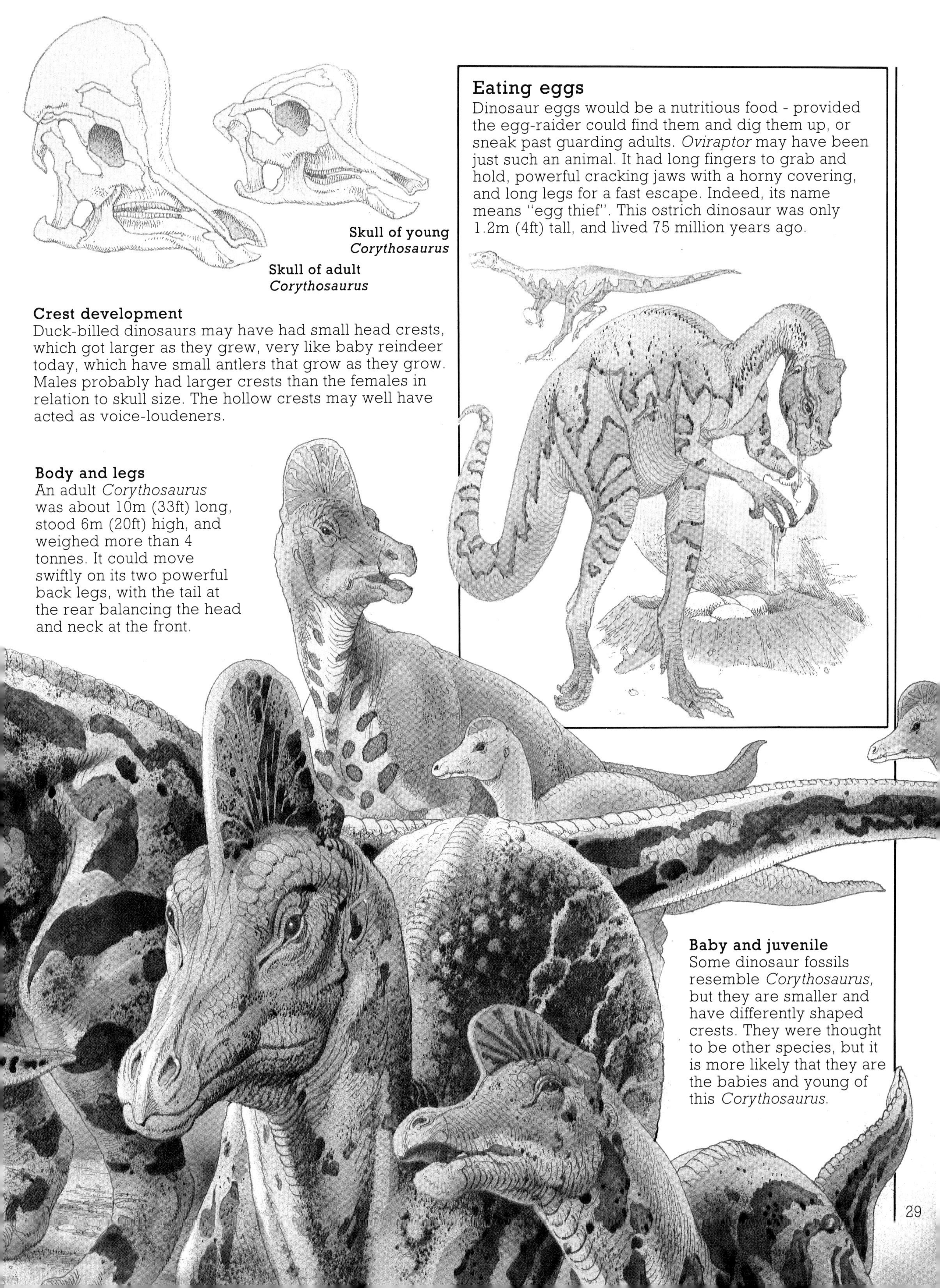

Crest development

Duck-billed dinosaurs may have had small head crests, which got larger as they grew, very like baby reindeer today, which have small antlers that grow as they grow. Males probably had larger crests than the females in relation to skull size. The hollow crests may well have acted as voice-loudeners.

Body and legs

An adult *Corythosaurus* was about 10m (33ft) long, stood 6m (20ft) high, and weighed more than 4 tonnes. It could move swiftly on its two powerful back legs, with the tail at the rear balancing the head and neck at the front.

Eating eggs

Dinosaur eggs would be a nutritious food - provided the egg-raider could find them and dig them up, or sneak past guarding adults. *Oviraptor* may have been just such an animal. It had long fingers to grab and hold, powerful cracking jaws with a horny covering, and long legs for a fast escape. Indeed, its name means "egg thief". This ostrich dinosaur was only 1.2m (4ft) tall, and lived 75 million years ago.

Baby and juvenile

Some dinosaur fossils resemble *Corythosaurus*, but they are smaller and have differently shaped crests. They were thought to be other species, but it is more likely that they are the babies and young of this *Corythosaurus*.

CLASH OF PERSONALITY

The largest flesh-eater ever to walk the earth was the massive dinosaur *Tyrannosaurus*. It lived in North America about 70-64 million years ago. With a length of 15m (49ft) and weighing perhaps 7 tonnes, its head was more than 5m (18ft) from the ground - so it could easily look into a first-floor window today! As this beast walked, it probably held its head low and its thick-based tail out behind as a counterweight. Despite its size and ferocious teeth, *Tyrannosaurus* may have been more of an ambusher and scavenger than an active hunter. It was probably too big and heavy to run long distances, and other dinosaurs of its day, such as *Ankylosaurus*, were heavily armoured and could put up a good fight. One puzzle is its tiny arms, which could not even reach its mouth for feeding. Maybe the arms were used, after lying down to rest, as an aid to getting up from the ground.

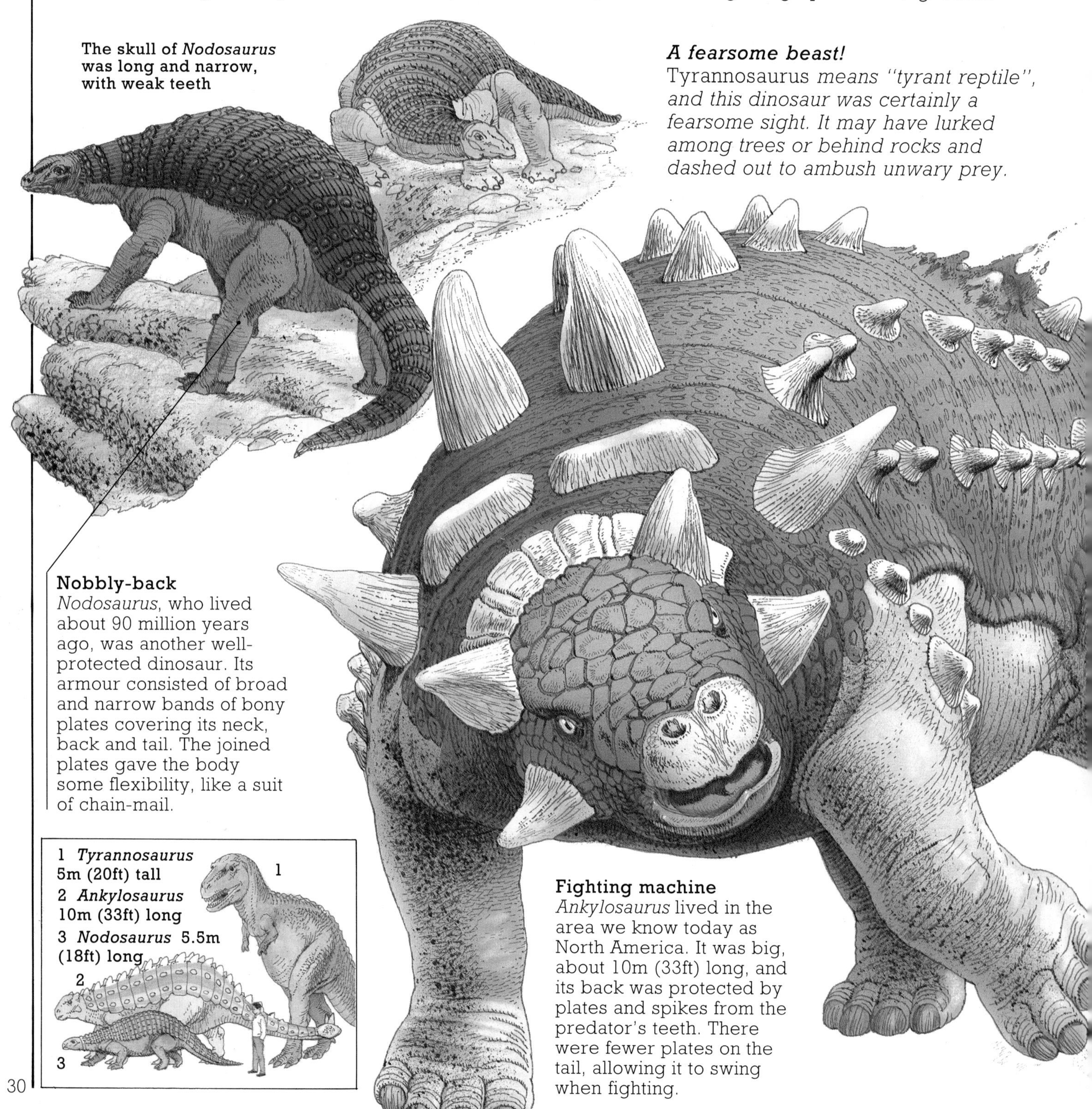

The skull of *Nodosaurus* was long and narrow, with weak teeth

A fearsome beast!
Tyrannosaurus *means "tyrant reptile", and this dinosaur was certainly a fearsome sight. It may have lurked among trees or behind rocks and dashed out to ambush unwary prey.*

Nobbly-back
Nodosaurus, who lived about 90 million years ago, was another well-protected dinosaur. Its armour consisted of broad and narrow bands of bony plates covering its neck, back and tail. The joined plates gave the body some flexibility, like a suit of chain-mail.

Fighting machine
Ankylosaurus lived in the area we know today as North America. It was big, about 10m (33ft) long, and its back was protected by plates and spikes from the predator's teeth. There were fewer plates on the tail, allowing it to swing when fighting.

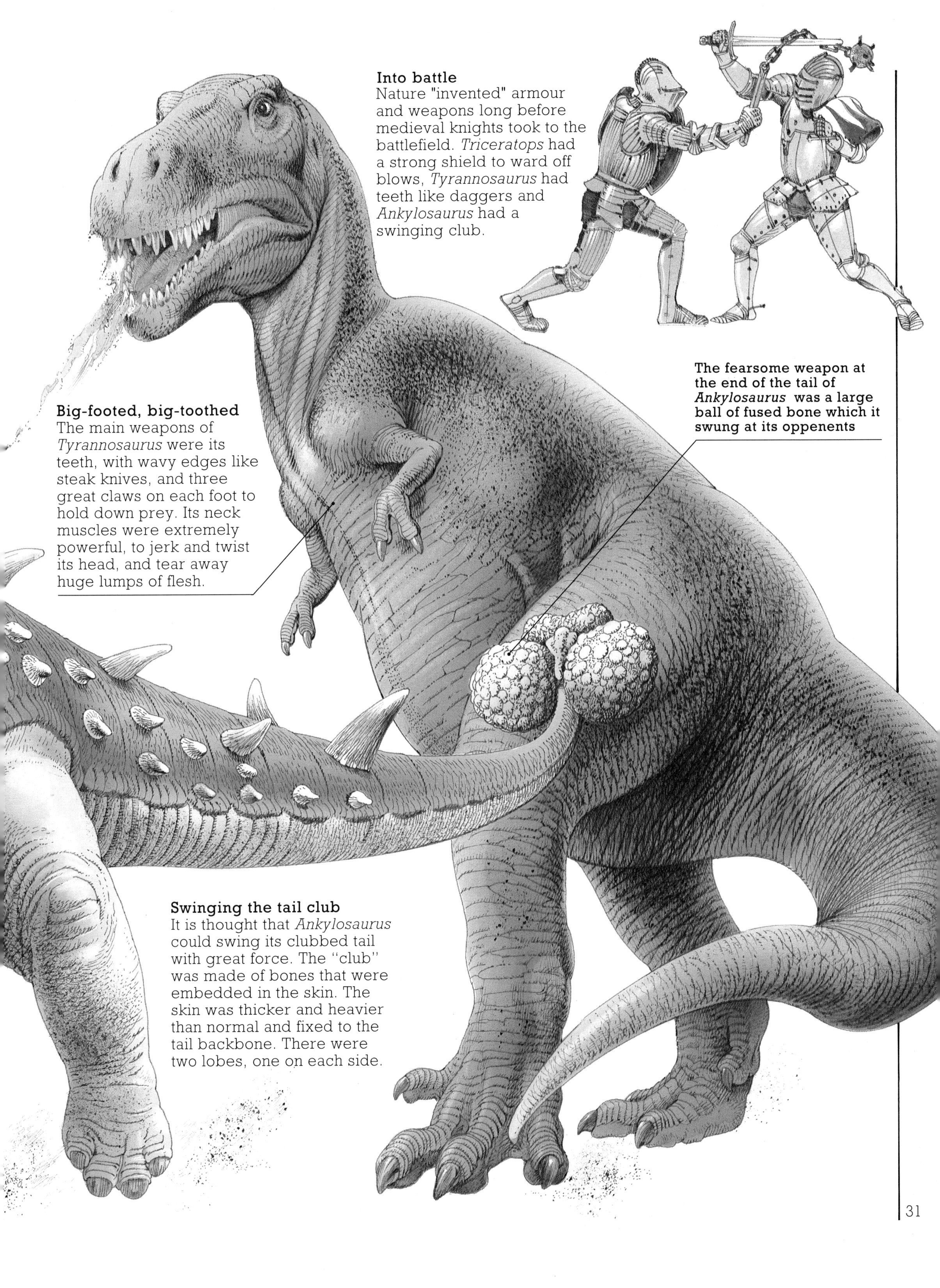
Into battle
Nature "invented" armour and weapons long before medieval knights took to the battlefield. *Triceratops* had a strong shield to ward off blows, *Tyrannosaurus* had teeth like daggers and *Ankylosaurus* had a swinging club.

Big-footed, big-toothed
The main weapons of *Tyrannosaurus* were its teeth, with wavy edges like steak knives, and three great claws on each foot to hold down prey. Its neck muscles were extremely powerful, to jerk and twist its head, and tear away huge lumps of flesh.

The fearsome weapon at the end of the tail of *Ankylosaurus* was a large ball of fused bone which it swung at its oppenents

Swinging the tail club
It is thought that *Ankylosaurus* could swing its clubbed tail with great force. The "club" was made of bones that were embedded in the skin. The skin was thicker and heavier than normal and fixed to the tail backbone. There were two lobes, one on each side.

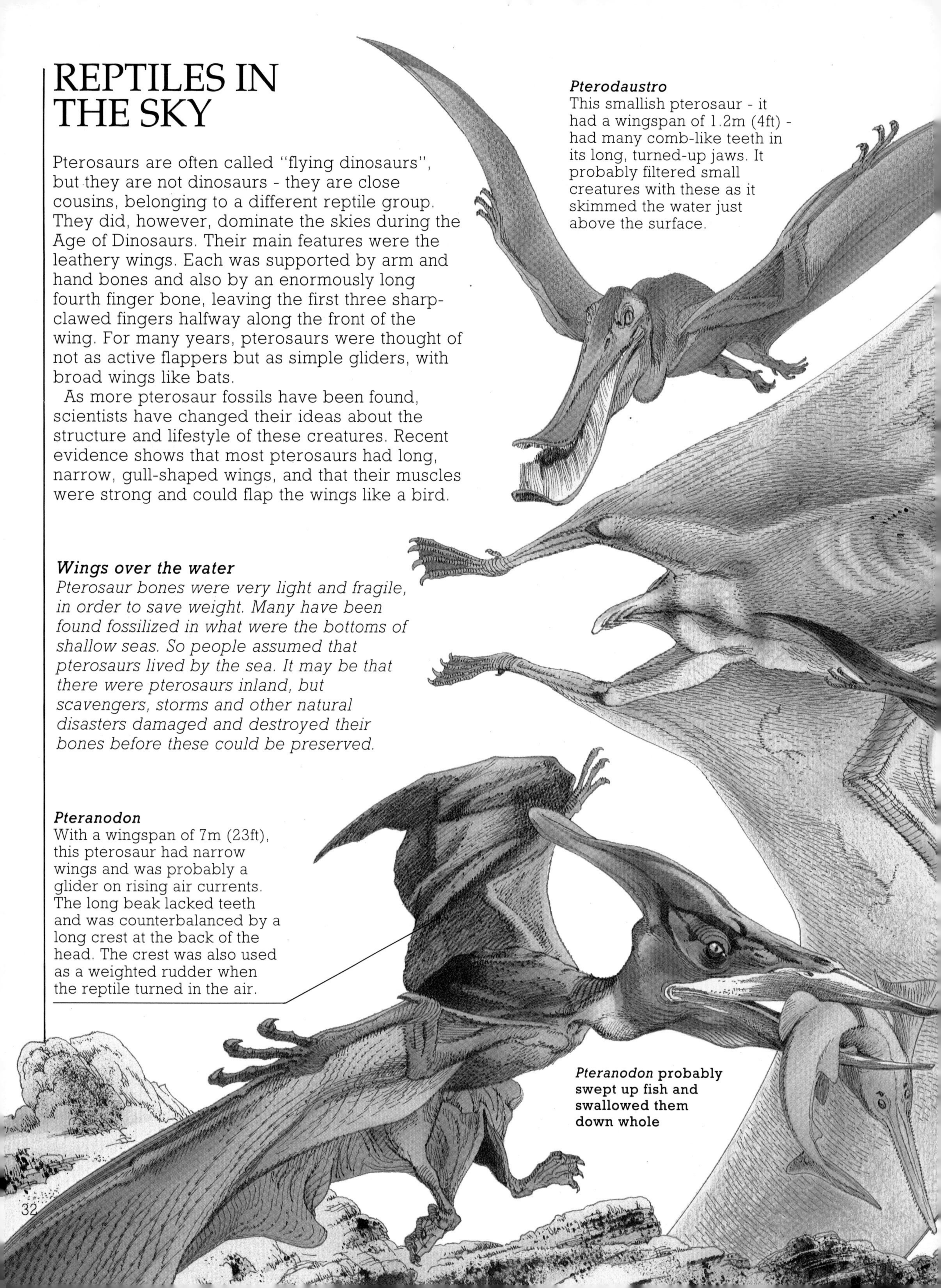

REPTILES IN THE SKY

Pterosaurs are often called "flying dinosaurs", but they are not dinosaurs - they are close cousins, belonging to a different reptile group. They did, however, dominate the skies during the Age of Dinosaurs. Their main features were the leathery wings. Each was supported by arm and hand bones and also by an enormously long fourth finger bone, leaving the first three sharp-clawed fingers halfway along the front of the wing. For many years, pterosaurs were thought of not as active flappers but as simple gliders, with broad wings like bats.

As more pterosaur fossils have been found, scientists have changed their ideas about the structure and lifestyle of these creatures. Recent evidence shows that most pterosaurs had long, narrow, gull-shaped wings, and that their muscles were strong and could flap the wings like a bird.

Pterodaustro
This smallish pterosaur - it had a wingspan of 1.2m (4ft) - had many comb-like teeth in its long, turned-up jaws. It probably filtered small creatures with these as it skimmed the water just above the surface.

Wings over the water
Pterosaur bones were very light and fragile, in order to save weight. Many have been found fossilized in what were the bottoms of shallow seas. So people assumed that pterosaurs lived by the sea. It may be that there were pterosaurs inland, but scavengers, storms and other natural disasters damaged and destroyed their bones before these could be preserved.

Pteranodon
With a wingspan of 7m (23ft), this pterosaur had narrow wings and was probably a glider on rising air currents. The long beak lacked teeth and was counterbalanced by a long crest at the back of the head. The crest was also used as a weighted rudder when the reptile turned in the air.

Pteranodon **probably swept up fish and swallowed them down whole**

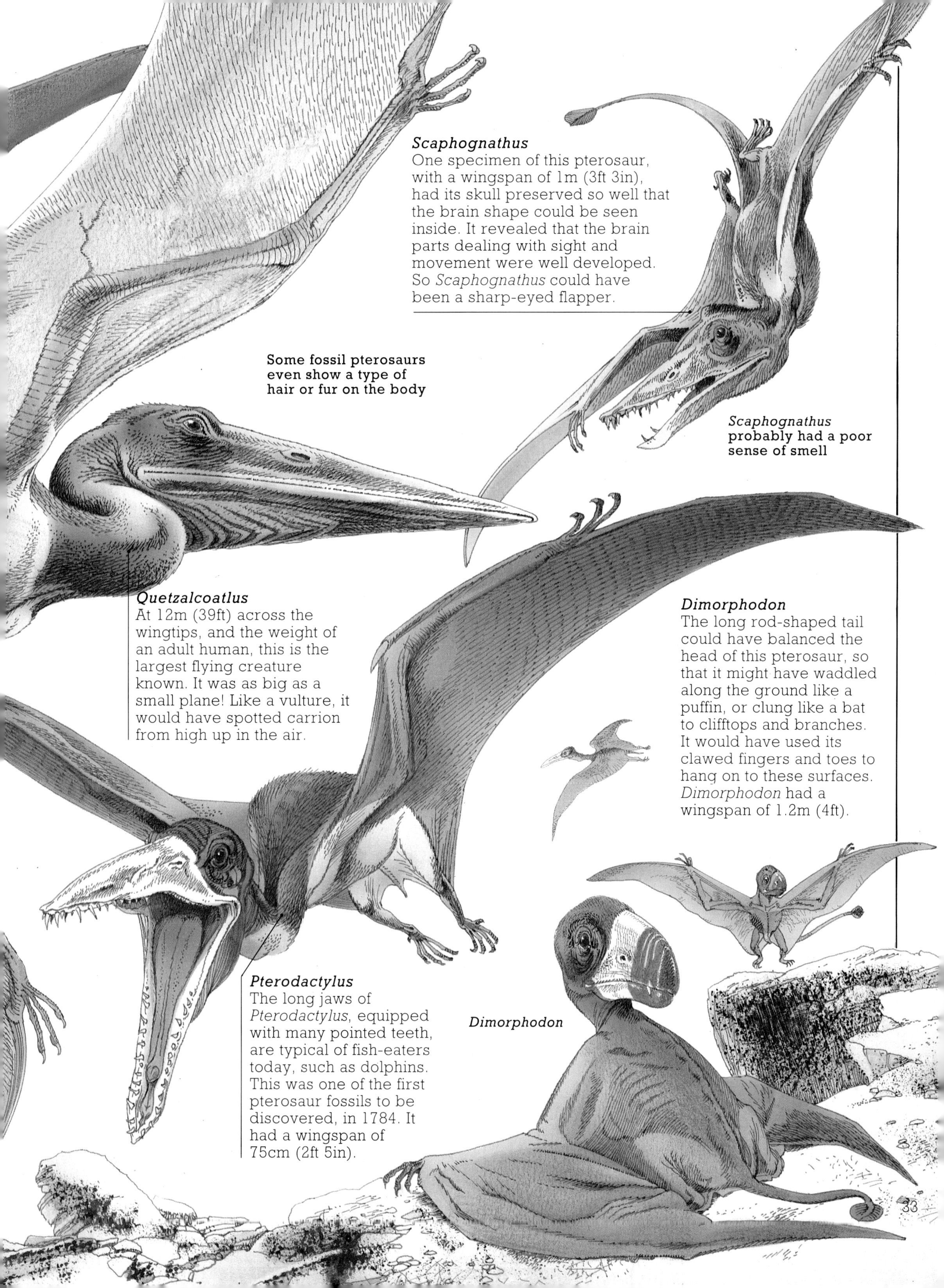

Scaphognathus
One specimen of this pterosaur, with a wingspan of 1m (3ft 3in), had its skull preserved so well that the brain shape could be seen inside. It revealed that the brain parts dealing with sight and movement were well developed. So *Scaphognathus* could have been a sharp-eyed flapper.

Some fossil pterosaurs even show a type of hair or fur on the body

***Scaphognathus* probably had a poor sense of smell**

Quetzalcoatlus
At 12m (39ft) across the wingtips, and the weight of an adult human, this is the largest flying creature known. It was as big as a small plane! Like a vulture, it would have spotted carrion from high up in the air.

Dimorphodon
The long rod-shaped tail could have balanced the head of this pterosaur, so that it might have waddled along the ground like a puffin, or clung like a bat to clifftops and branches. It would have used its clawed fingers and toes to hang on to these surfaces. *Dimorphodon* had a wingspan of 1.2m (4ft).

Pterodactylus
The long jaws of *Pterodactylus*, equipped with many pointed teeth, are typical of fish-eaters today, such as dolphins. This was one of the first pterosaur fossils to be discovered, in 1784. It had a wingspan of 75cm (2ft 5in).

Dimorphodon

UNCOVERING THE TRUTH

The exciting museum displays of prehistoric plants and animals are the result of years of hard work by many teams of experts. Fossils are often found halfway up a mountain or in a stony desert - not ideal places to work. The first task is to extract and partly clean the sections of the find, as shown here, and transport them safely from the site. With a big discovery, many tonnes of rock must be hacked away - and sometimes small explosions have to be set off. The detailed work is done in the cleaner, more comfortable conditions of the paleontology laboratory (pages 36-37).

In the field

It takes many weeks to dig up the fossils of a large creature such as this Archelon, *a turtle that lived at the same time as the dinosaurs. Its thick 3m (10ft) long shell was good protection against sea predators such as mosasaurs (page 38).*

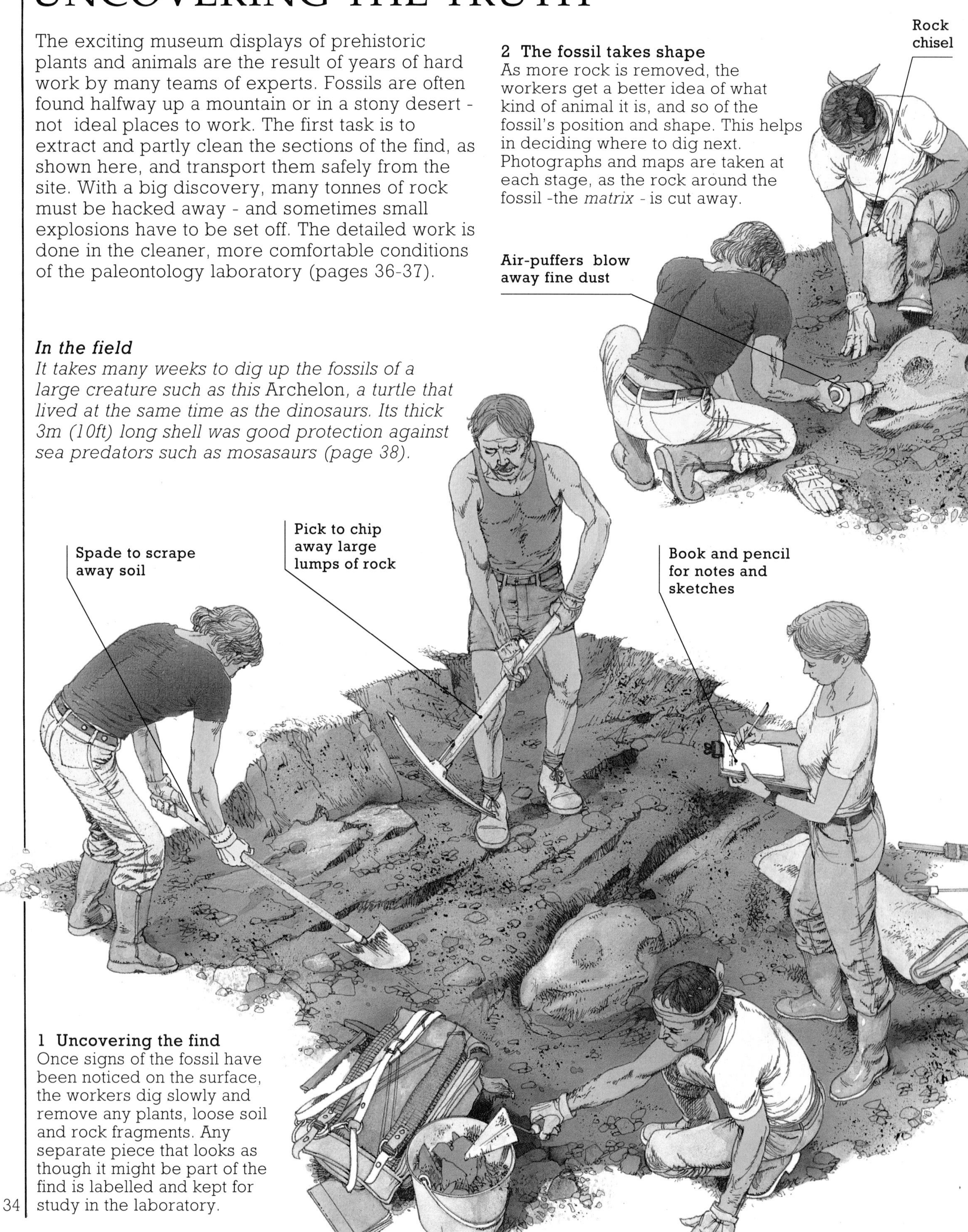

2 The fossil takes shape
As more rock is removed, the workers get a better idea of what kind of animal it is, and so of the fossil's position and shape. This helps in deciding where to dig next. Photographs and maps are taken at each stage, as the rock around the fossil -the *matrix* - is cut away.

1 Uncovering the find
Once signs of the fossil have been noticed on the surface, the workers dig slowly and remove any plants, loose soil and rock fragments. Any separate piece that looks as though it might be part of the find is labelled and kept for study in the laboratory.

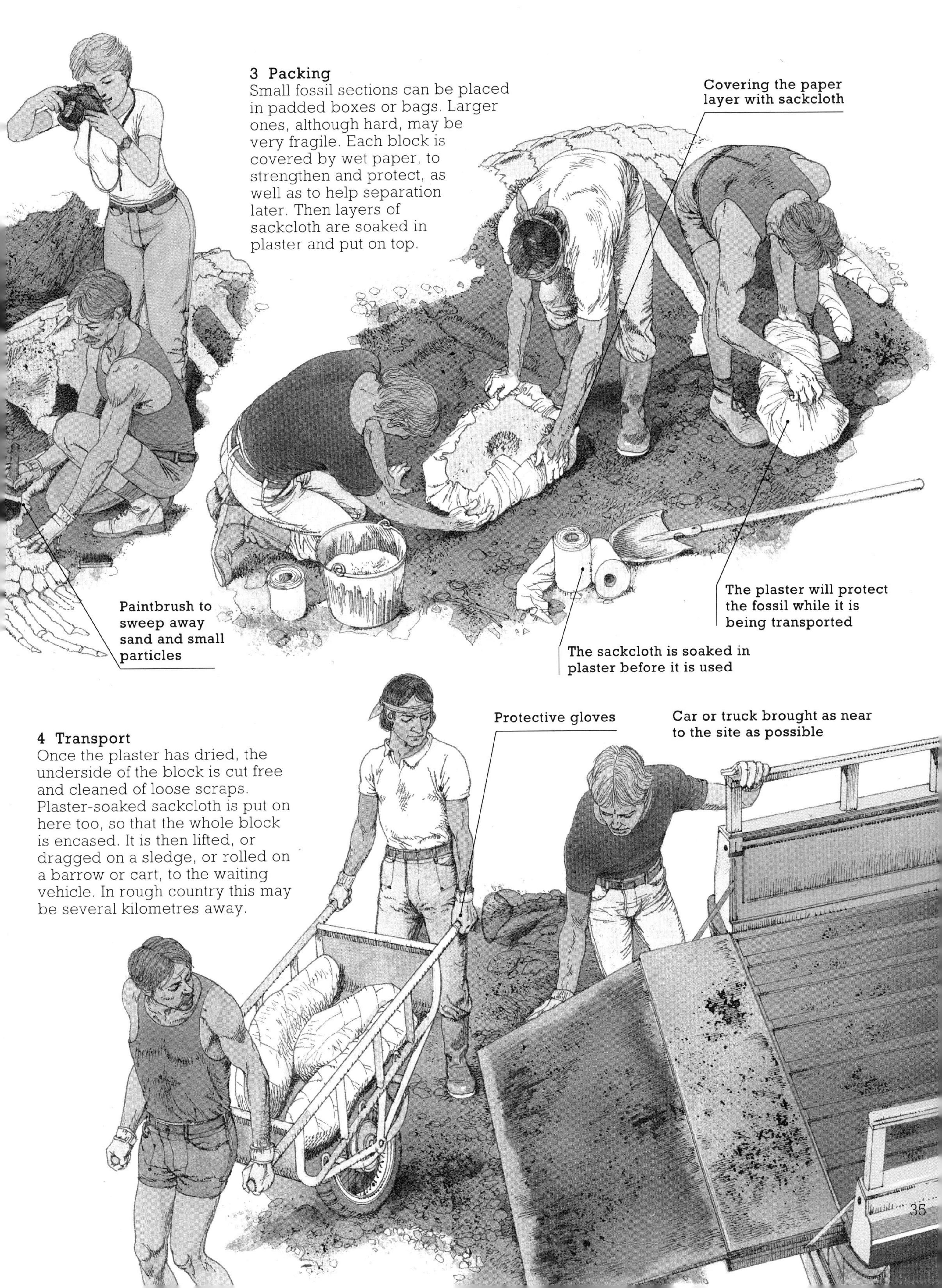

3 Packing
Small fossil sections can be placed in padded boxes or bags. Larger ones, although hard, may be very fragile. Each block is covered by wet paper, to strengthen and protect, as well as to help separation later. Then layers of sackcloth are soaked in plaster and put on top.

4 Transport
Once the plaster has dried, the underside of the block is cut free and cleaned of loose scraps. Plaster-soaked sackcloth is put on here too, so that the whole block is encased. It is then lifted, or dragged on a sledge, or rolled on a barrow or cart, to the waiting vehicle. In rough country this may be several kilometres away.

In the laboratory

Once the carefully packed blocks reach the laboratory, the delicate and painstaking work of cleaning and reassembly begins. This may take years. Preparators remove the rest of the rock with great care. They try not to damage the fossil's surface, since nicks and scratches can be confused with the natural ridges where muscles and other bones were attached.

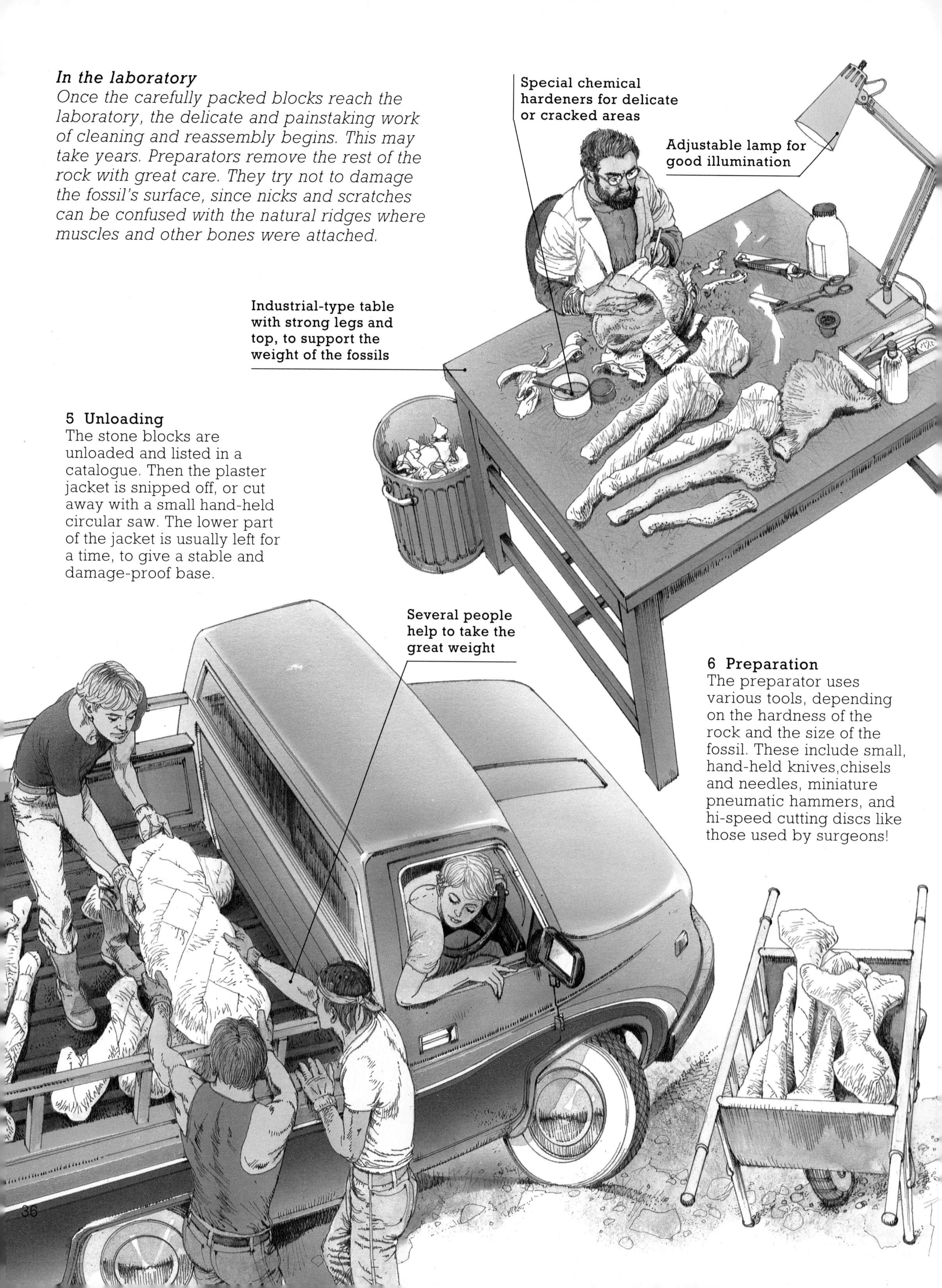

5 Unloading

The stone blocks are unloaded and listed in a catalogue. Then the plaster jacket is snipped off, or cut away with a small hand-held circular saw. The lower part of the jacket is usually left for a time, to give a stable and damage-proof base.

6 Preparation

The preparator uses various tools, depending on the hardness of the rock and the size of the fossil. These include small, hand-held knives,chisels and needles, miniature pneumatic hammers, and hi-speed cutting discs like those used by surgeons!

7 Recording

After the fossil is extracted and repaired, it is drawn from various angles by an expert scientific illustrator. A good line drawing can emphasize details that the camera may miss, and it will also print more clearly in books and scientific journals.

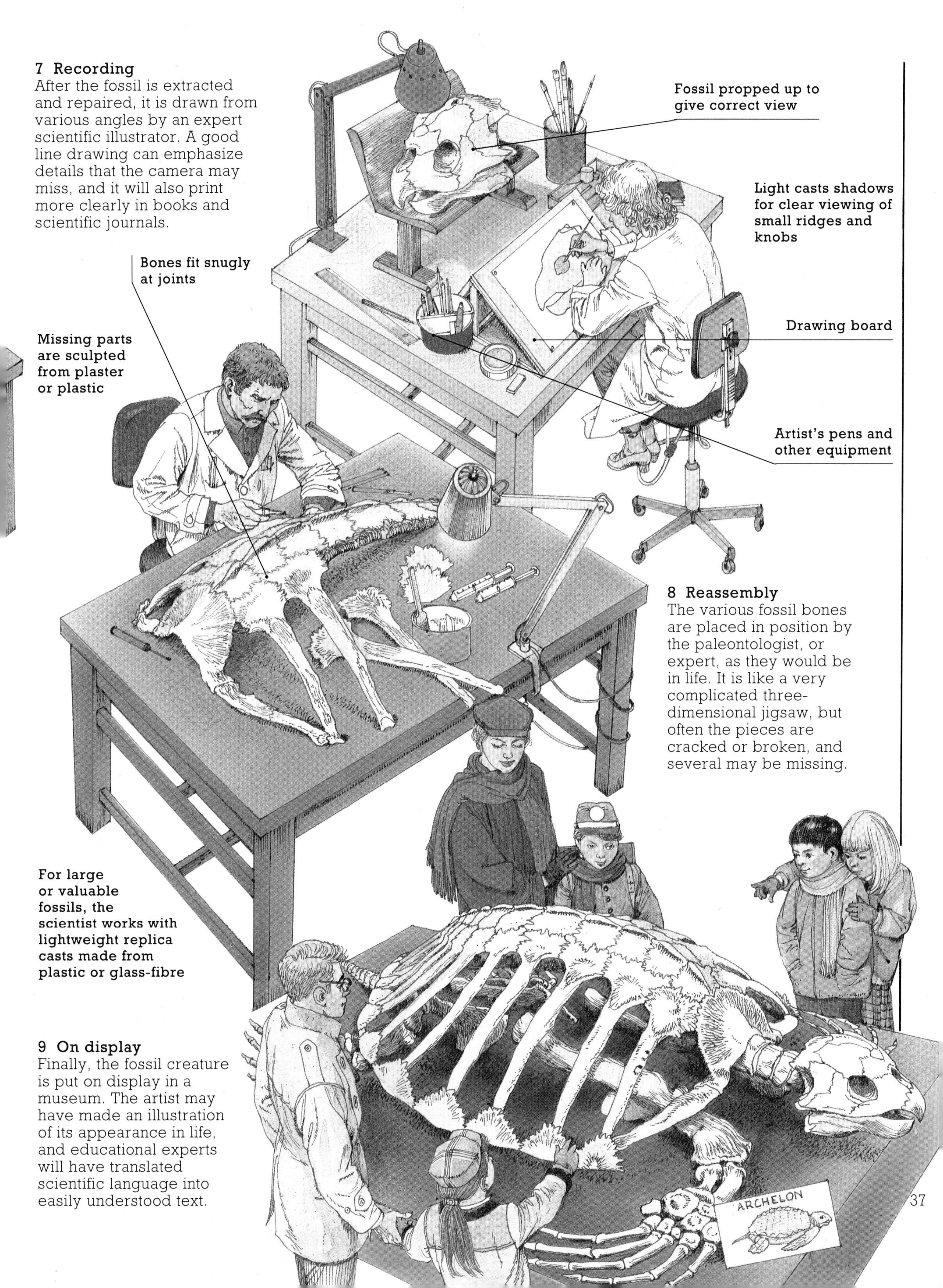

8 Reassembly

The various fossil bones are placed in position by the paleontologist, or expert, as they would be in life. It is like a very complicated three-dimensional jigsaw, but often the pieces are cracked or broken, and several may be missing.

9 On display

Finally, the fossil creature is put on display in a museum. The artist may have made an illustration of its appearance in life, and educational experts will have translated scientific language into easily understood text.

IN ANCIENT SEAS

Until 64 million years ago, many kinds of large and fearsome reptiles lived in the sea. Most died out along with the dinosaurs, leaving only crocodiles and turtles as the water-dwelling reptiles of the present. Besides those shown here, there were several other groups. Placodonts, which looked like big lizards, fed on shellfish by plucking them from the sea bed with pincer-like front teeth before crushing the shells with flattened back teeth. Mosasaurs were gigantic "sea lizards", 10m (33ft) long with sharp fangs. They are related to today's monitor lizards, and they became plentiful towards the end of the Age of Dinosaurs. Even so, they could not survive the great extinction (page 55).

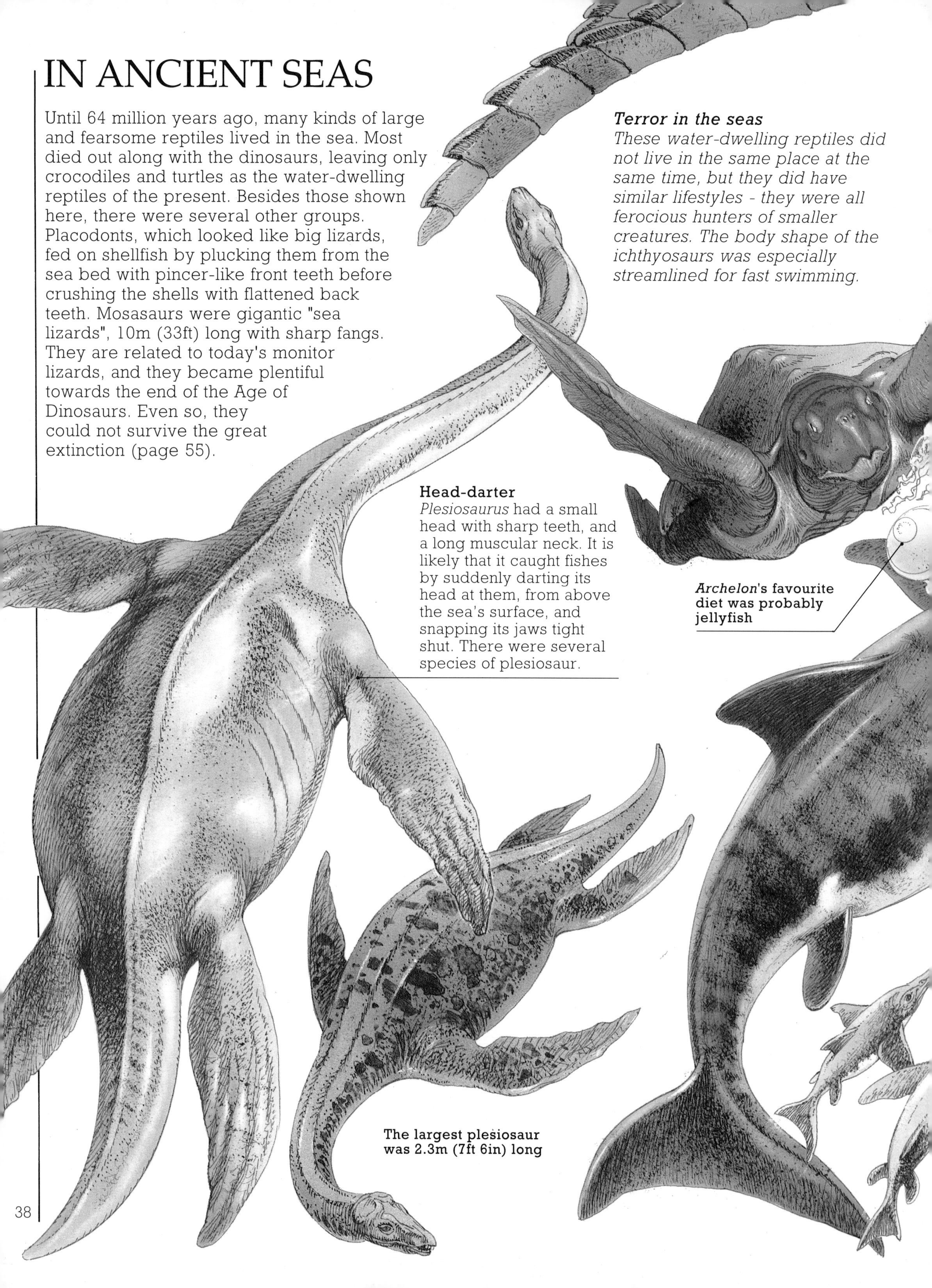

Terror in the seas
These water-dwelling reptiles did not live in the same place at the same time, but they did have similar lifestyles - they were all ferocious hunters of smaller creatures. The body shape of the ichthyosaurs was especially streamlined for fast swimming.

Head-darter
Plesiosaurus had a small head with sharp teeth, and a long muscular neck. It is likely that it caught fishes by suddenly darting its head at them, from above the sea's surface, and snapping its jaws tight shut. There were several species of plesiosaur.

***Archelon*'s favourite diet was probably jellyfish**

The largest plesiosaur was 2.3m (7ft 6in) long

Jellyfish-chewer
Archelon was a huge sea-living turtle (see also pages 34-37). It had a hard, hooked "beak" and large, strong flippers with which it paddled through the water. Although it had weak jaws and no teeth, it may have been able to crunch through the shells of shellfish.

Squid-snatcher
Ichthyosaurus was suited to life in the water, like the dolphin of today. In some fossils, the remains of meals have been preserved and show that they ate fishes, squid and pterosaurs. They also reveal that these reptiles did not lay eggs, but gave birth to fully-formed babies.

Newly-born ichthyosaurs

Dinosaur-diner
The terrifying *Deinosuchus* lived in fresh water, and probably ventured onto land as well. The crocodile may have ambushed wading dinosaurs or those coming to drink. It is the largest crocodile ever discovered, with a skull 2m (6ft 6in) long and a body length of 15m (49ft).

EARLY SPRING

Our world today is dominated by flowering plants - the Angiosperms or "enclosed seed" plants, whose seeds are contained in a protective covering which may form a fruit or nut. They range from flowers such as orchids, buttercups and roses, to herbs and shrubs like sage and privet, to oaks, maples, beeches and other great trees. About 110 million years ago there were hardly any flowering plants, the main vegetation being Gymnosperms ("naked seed" plants) such as conifer trees and cycads, as well as seed ferns and mosses. Yet by 90 million years ago, fossils of wood and pollen reveal that many flowering plant groups had appeared.

Bursting into flower
Flowering plants evolved rapidly during the "prehistoric springtime" of 100 million years ago. Their fossils are rare, so reconstructions are made mainly by working backwards from today's groups. Angiosperms now make up more than four-fifths of living plant species.

Head-banging contests
About this time, the first members of the pachycephalosaur dinosaur group appeared. Their name means "thick-headed reptiles" and they had very thick bone on the top of the skull. They may have held head-butting competitions to win mates or territory.

Magnolia

Hiding in the boughs
Alphadon was a marsupial mammal, an opossum-like creature about 30cm (1ft) in long, with gripping toes and a long tail. It probably lived in trees and ate small creatures as well as the new foods of flowers and fruits.

Cycads
Fewer than 100 species of cycads survive from this once-great plant group. They resemble palms and are found in tropical regions. Cycads appeared during Permian times and faded as flowering trees took over.

Tall as a tree fern
Tree ferns are tall, woody cousins of low-growing ferns such as bracken. In prehistoric times they grew in vast forests to heights of 18m (60ft). They still do now - tree ferns survive in the tropics, although they are much less common.

Volcanoes
In the late Cretaceous period, the Earth's continents had split up and were beginning to drift to their present positions. Volcanic eruptions and earthquakes would have been common in some parts of the world.

A new partnership
Flowers gave insects opportunities to evolve. Flies, bees and butterflies could be used to carry pollen from one flower to another, to fertilize its eggs and so form seeds. Some flowers developed sugary nectar to entice insects to their pollen.

Small meals
The tiny mammal *Purgatorius* is known only from its fossil teeth, which indicate it was one of the first primates (the mammal group including monkeys, apes and humans). With a length estimate at only 10cm (4in), its likely prey was worms, insects and similar creatures.

BIRDS OF A FEATHER

As dinosaurs walked along an ancient seashore, a strange feathered creature flew out over a shallow lagoon. For some reason it plunged into the water, died and sank to the bottom. The water was so lacking in oxygen and salty that few animals lived there, so the dead creature was not torn apart by scavengers. Gradually, fine particles settled over its remains, and they were lost from sight. Then, 140 million years later, a worker in a German quarry split open a piece of limestone to reveal the same creature, beautifully fossilized. It is *Archaeopteryx*, the first known bird, and a strange half-way combination of features from both reptiles and modern birds. The key feature is the feather: any animal that possesses feathers must be a bird.

Dragonfly dinner

Archaeopteryx *may have perched among scattered tree-like plants, from which it could swoop after insects and other small creatures. It could probably fly, but not as powerfully as a bird of today. It would have caught most of the insects it ate on the wing.*

Toothed beak

Unlike any bird now alive, *Archaeopteryx* had small, spiky teeth in its beak. These were probably a leftover from its reptile ancestry. However, they would also have been useful for gripping struggling prey.

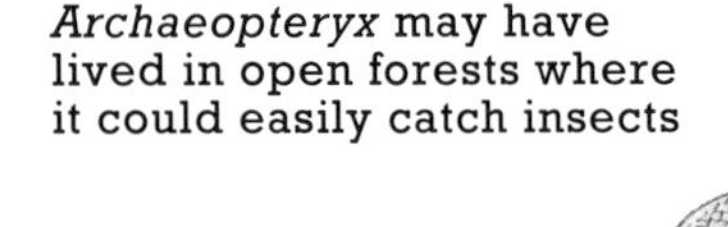

***Archaeopteryx* may have lived in open forests where it could easily catch insects**

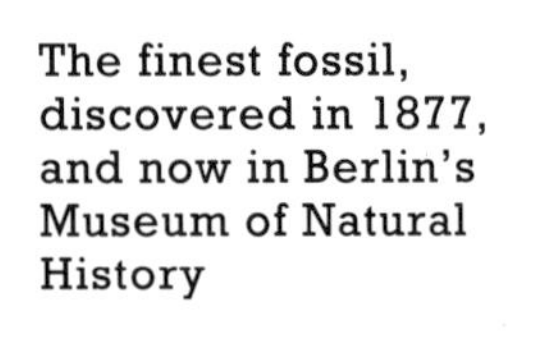

The finest fossil, discovered in 1877, and now in Berlin's Museum of Natural History

Famous fossil

The first *Archaeopteryx* fossil was found in 1861 in a quarry at Solnhofen, Germany. The limestone there is very fine-grained, so it preserved the bones and feathers in amazing detail. Since then, five more *Archaeopteryx* fossils have come to light. One was first thought to be a pterosaur, and another was mistaken for the small dinosaur *Compsognathus*.

The breastbone,or sternum, was tiny, unlike that of the birds of today, and may mean that *Archaeopteryx* was a better glider than a flier

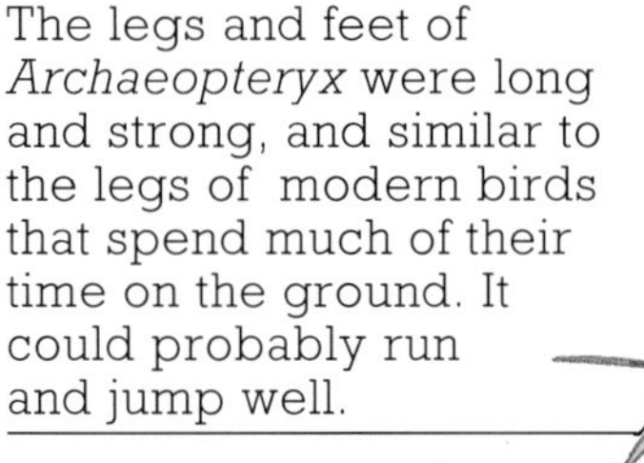

Clawed feet

The legs and feet of *Archaeopteryx* were long and strong, and similar to the legs of modern birds that spend much of their time on the ground. It could probably run and jump well.

Fish supper

Fossils of *Ichthyornis* were discovered in North America about 10 years after those of *Archaeopteryx*. This bird probably dived for fish like a modern tern. It is the first bird known to have a strong breastbone with a flange or keel, which anchored the wing-flapping muscles.

Ichthyornis was a strong flyer

Clawed wings

With the exception of the hoatzin, present-day birds have lost the claws on their wings. Otherwise, the wings are very similar to those of today's birds, with large feathers that give a broad, airtight surface for effective flight.

Spot the difference

Archaeopteryx's skeleton is similar to that of a small two-legged dinosaur such as *Compsognathus*. This is good evidence that birds and dinosaurs shared common ancestors. Since then, birds have developed a large breastbone.

Long back legs for running; long, flexible neck and tail

Arm-like front limbs; bony tail; no breastbone

Tail bones lost; large breastbone; no claws on wings

NEW FACES

Mammals and birds lived in the shadows of the great dinosaurs for millions of years. Soon after the Age of Dinosaurs ended mysteriously, 64 million years ago, they began to develop rapidly into a variety of novel and strange forms. New groups of mammals evolved and spread across the world. For example, the creodonts were the main flesh-eating mammals from about 60 to 30 million years ago, and some survived to 10 million years ago. They were widespread and ranged from the size of weasels and domestic cats, through members similar to foxes and wolves, to giants larger than any big cat or bear alive now. The creodonts had small brains and their teeth were not as well suited to tearing flesh as those of a cat or dog. Gradually the modern carnivores - weasels, cats, foxes, wolves and bears - took over, and the creodonts died away.

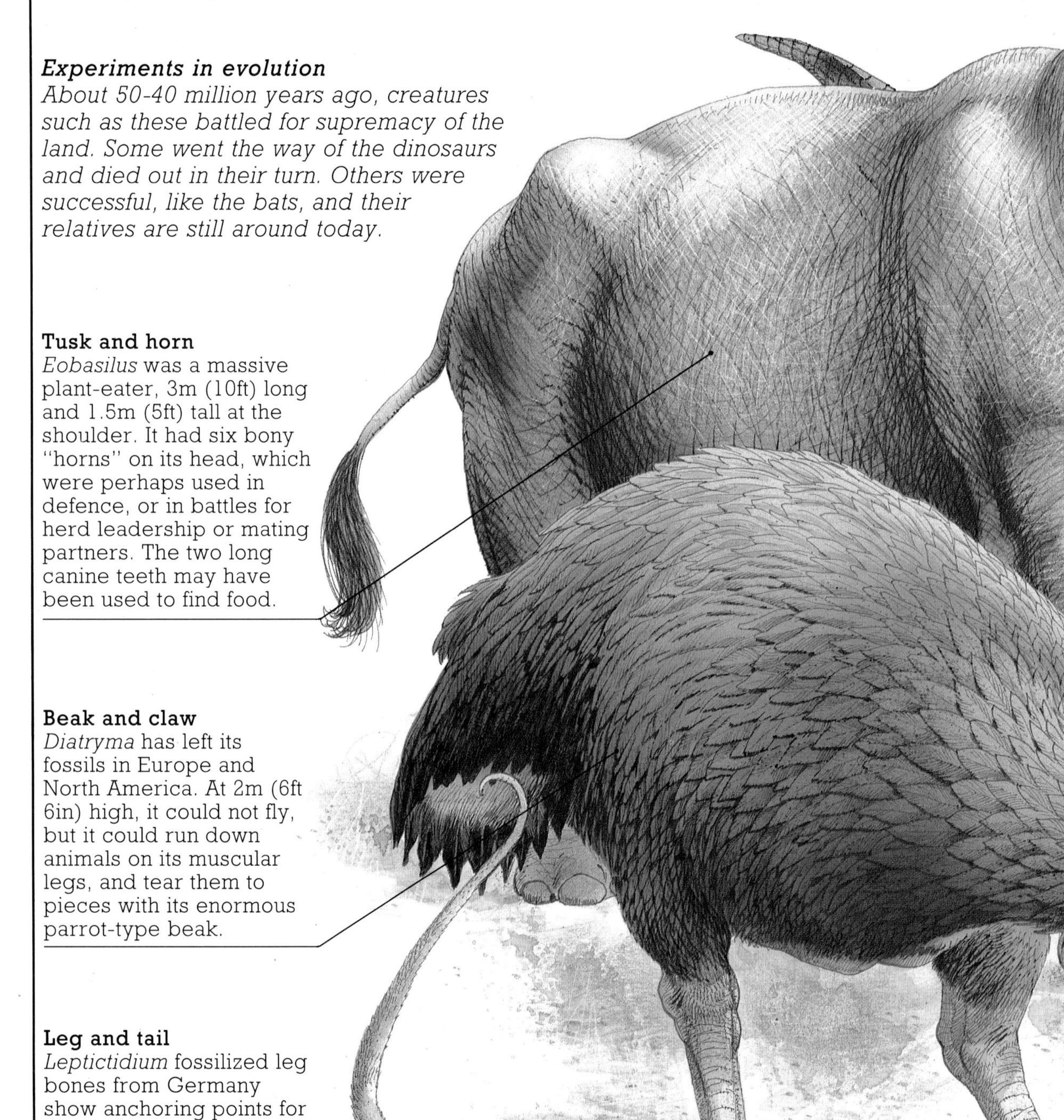

Experiments in evolution
About 50-40 million years ago, creatures such as these battled for supremacy of the land. Some went the way of the dinosaurs and died out in their turn. Others were successful, like the bats, and their relatives are still around today.

Tusk and horn
Eobasilus was a massive plant-eater, 3m (10ft) long and 1.5m (5ft) tall at the shoulder. It had six bony "horns" on its head, which were perhaps used in defence, or in battles for herd leadership or mating partners. The two long canine teeth may have been used to find food.

Beak and claw
Diatryma has left its fossils in Europe and North America. At 2m (6ft 6in) high, it could not fly, but it could run down animals on its muscular legs, and tear them to pieces with its enormous parrot-type beak.

Leg and tail
Leptictidium fossilized leg bones from Germany show anchoring points for strong thigh muscles, indicating a fast, two-legged runner. It was 75 cm (2ft 5in) long and ate insects, little lizards and small mammals.

Icaronycteris was very like the bats of today

Wing and skin
Icaronycteris, the earliest known bat, probably roosted upside down and caught insects in flight. Its wings were quite short compared to most modern bats, and its tail was long and lacked the web of skin attaching it to the legs.

Jaw and claw
Sarkastodon was a giant among creodonts, 3m (10ft) long, with a heavily-built, bear-like body. It had massive jaws but its teeth were not particularly specialized. This indicates it ate various kinds of food, like the bears of today.

Seize and chop
It is thought that the creodont *Hyaenodon* both hunted and scavenged on other animals, like the hyaena of today. Its long fangs seized prey, and its sharp cheek teeth were fairly good at shearing flesh and chopping gristle.

Hoof and tooth
Pristichampsus was a crocodile, one of the few groups of large reptiles that survived the dinosaur-destroying disaster. It was 3m (10ft) long and had long legs for running. It used its saw-edged teeth to slice up the evolving and abundant mammals.

SEAS OF GRASS

About 30 million years after the disappearance of the Dinosaurs, the mammals had evolved into many different shapes and sizes, from tiny shrews on land to huge whales in the oceans. But during the Miocene epoch, from about 25 million years ago, there was a change in the Earth's climate. Gradually it became drier. The seas shrank in some areas, and because of the buckling and tilting of the Earth's crust, the Mediterranean Sea almost disappeared. This change in climate had an effect on plants. Moisture-loving woodlands with their leafy trees slowly shrank, to be replaced by smaller, tougher plants which could cope with drought - the grasses. As the plants evolved, so did the animals that fed on them, and so did the predators that hunted these herbivores.

The graceful 3-toed grazing horse, *Hipparion*, survived until about two million years ago

Grazers on the grasslands

Miocene times saw the development of many sharp-eyed, long-legged herbivores, ready to detect and escape from predators on the open plains. Some were from the horse group, like Hipparion, *shown here. Others were kinds of giraffes, pigs, deers and camels.*

Manes and tails

The horse's long tail is a useful whisk to swish away pesky flies. It is also, along with the mane and ears, a signalling device to inform other herd members at a distance about an animal's moods and intentions. The ears, like the eyes, were on top of the head for good all-round hearing.

Disappearing toes

The horse story is one of losing toes. Early members like *Hyracotherium* had four toes on each front foot and three on each back one. By about 20 million years ago *Merychippus* had only one main toe on each foot, capped with a large hoof, while the other two had become small side toes. Modern horses have one toe on each foot. This saves weight, is stronger, and makes it easier to swing the limb fast when running.

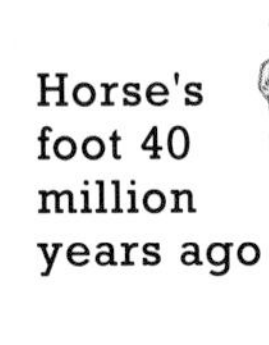

Horse's foot 40 million years ago

Horse's foot 20 million years ago

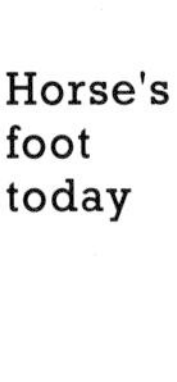

Horse's foot today

Eyes on top

In open country, keen senses of sight and smell are needed to spot mates, rivals and danger. The eyes of grassland animals became wide-set and near the top of the head, for all-round vision. They were large too, to see predators hunting at twilight or night.

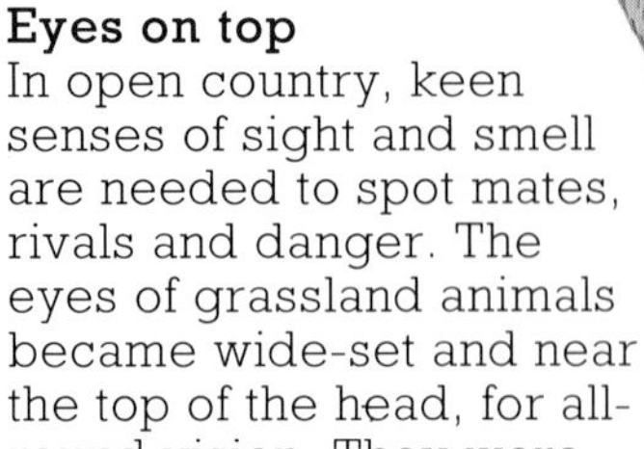

Camels and pronghorns

Some animal groups which have only a few members today, were numerous and varied on the Miocene prairies. There are only a few present-day species in the camel group, but *Aepycamelus,* also known as *Alticamelus,* was one of the many prehistoric forms. It stood 3m (10ft) tall, with long legs and neck. Only one kind of pronghorn survives, yet the 1.8m (6ft) long *Ilingoceros* and several other kinds lived during the Miocene.

Grass-raspers

The cheek teeth of the grazers were broad and long, and had ridged surfaces. These were adapted for chewing and crushing the tough grass leaves and stems, in order to break them open and extract the sap and nutrients for digestion.

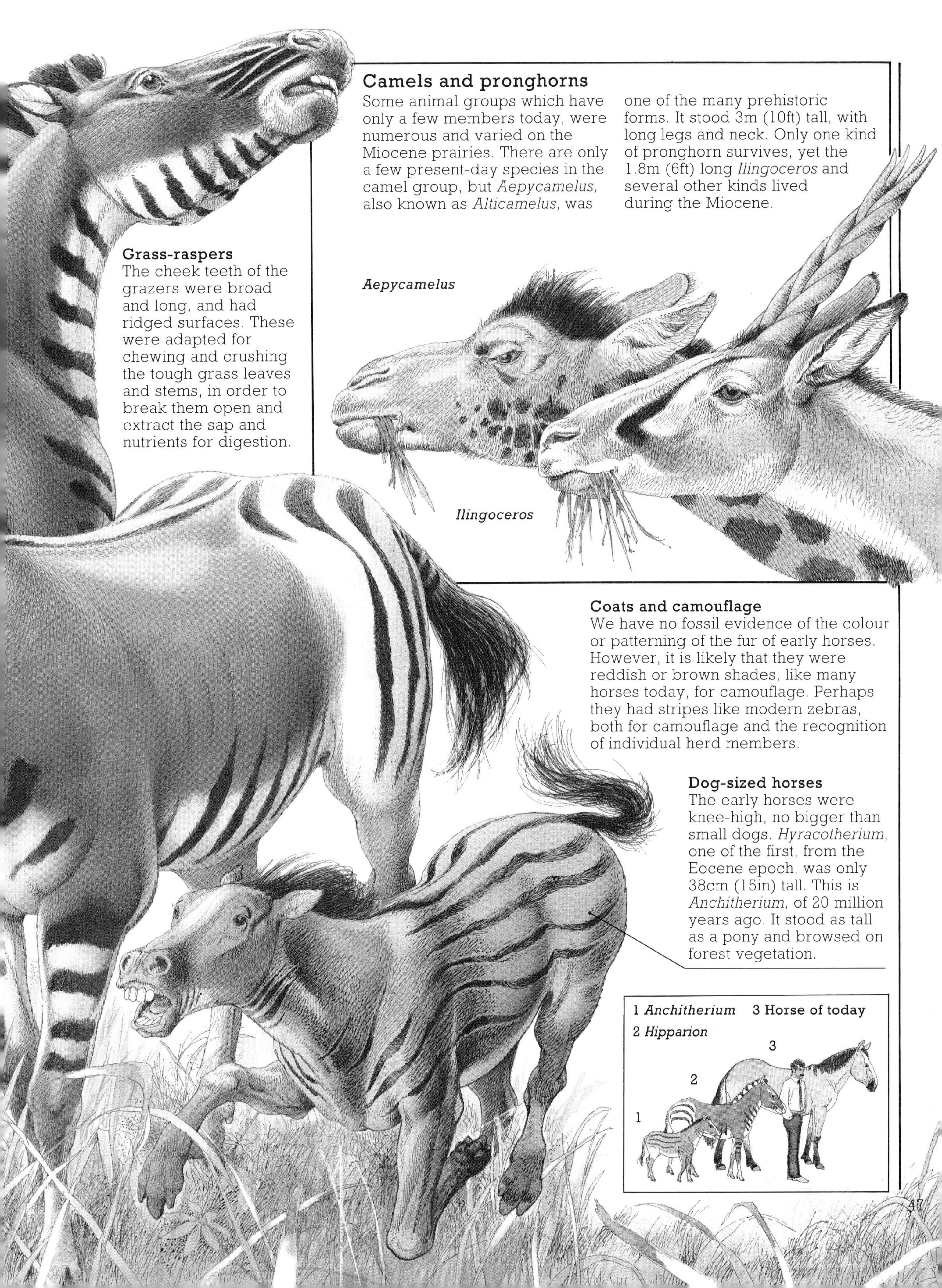

Coats and camouflage

We have no fossil evidence of the colour or patterning of the fur of early horses. However, it is likely that they were reddish or brown shades, like many horses today, for camouflage. Perhaps they had stripes like modern zebras, both for camouflage and the recognition of individual herd members.

Dog-sized horses

The early horses were knee-high, no bigger than small dogs. *Hyracotherium*, one of the first, from the Eocene epoch, was only 38cm (15in) tall. This is *Anchitherium*, of 20 million years ago. It stood as tall as a pony and browsed on forest vegetation.

THE ICE AGES

The past two million years, the Pleistocene epoch, have seen a cooling-down of the Earth's climate. This is shown by the types of rocks formed, and the kinds of plants and animals fossilized. There have also been at least four much colder periods in the past 700,000 years. During these "Ice Ages" or Glacials, the glaciers and ice sheets spread outwards from the North and South Poles. The ice reached south to Texas in the USA and France in Europe. At times, it covered half the planet's land surface. Then the climate warmed and the ice melted back, bringing an interval called an Interglacial.

From warm to cold
As the climate cooled over several thousand years, the landscapes of central North America and Western Europe would have changed dramatically. The warm, subtropical plains of the Interglacial would give way to the snow and bitter cold of the Ice Age. These changes happened so slowly that most plants and animals had time to adapt and move to more suitable areas.

Modern people (*Homo sapiens sapiens*)

Early victims
During Interglacials, the extinct rhino *Dicerorhinus* wandered across central Europe. Such animals would have been easy prey for bands of marauding humans, who may have contributed to their disappearance - along with the returning ice and cold.

Dry-plains drifters
Today's two hippo species are tropical water-lovers and live only in Africa. But during the past, many other hippo species lived in forest and grassland habitats. During the warm Interglacials, they spread north across the Channel land bridge into Britain.

Plants
Before the ice returned, warmth-loving subtropical plants thrived. Fossilized microscopic pollen grains, leaves, twigs and stems have been found. These show which grasses and herbs, now common in Mediterranean countries, grew in Northern Europe.

The biggest deer
The largest deer was the "Irish elk", *Megaloceros,* which grew antlers more than 3.7m (12ft) across. More like a fallow deer than an elk, it lived not only in Ireland, but was widespread across Europe during the last Interglacial.

The moving ice front
As each Glacial period began, the ice front moved south at about 100m (330ft) each year. In North America, the giant bison, whose horn-span was more than 2m (6ft 6in), would have been forced to migrate southwards.

Arctic Mid-Europe
The Arctic animals that roamed Europe included reindeers, lemmings, and Arctic foxes. During the worst weather the well-named cave bear of Europe sheltered in caves, where many of its bones have been found.

TOOTH AND CLAW

There are no sabre-toothed cats alive today. But through the Age of Mammals, various predators have evolved huge, curved, blade-like front teeth for stabbing and slashing victims. From Oligocene times the cat group, in particular, has come up with sabre-toothed representatives.

One of the first sabre-tooths was *Hoplophoneus*, whose 35-million-year-old fossils have been found in North America. *Machairodus* was another example from 10 million years ago. It looked like a lion, with powerful legs and a stubby tail. A remarkably similar species is known from remains preserved in tar pits in western North America. This is *Smilodon*, which evolved more than two million years ago, yet died out perhaps only 10,000 years ago. Possibly humans had a hand in its disappearance.

The leap of death

With an upward leap and a downward lunge, Smilodon *attempts to stab a dire wolf, an extinct wolf similar to today's grey wolf. This may have been defensive behaviour, as the sabre-toothed cat tries to drive away the pack of dire wolves, to prevent them from stealing its kill.*

***Smilodon* was as big as a modern leopard**

Mouth closed

Sabre-tooths through the ages have had remarkably similar dental and jaw designs. The main teeth curved down and back, and were outside the mouth when this was closed. There was a downward-facing projection of the lower jawbone behind the teeth, which may have helped to support them and stop them from snapping off.

Neck and legs

Smilodon's neck and front limbs were muscular and powerful. It probably held down prey with its front claws and then stabbed with its teeth, jabbing with its neck and head. It may have cut the prey's neck arteries and then left it to bleed to death.

1 **Dire wolf 2m (6ft 6in) long**
2 ***Smilodon* 1.2m (4ft) long**

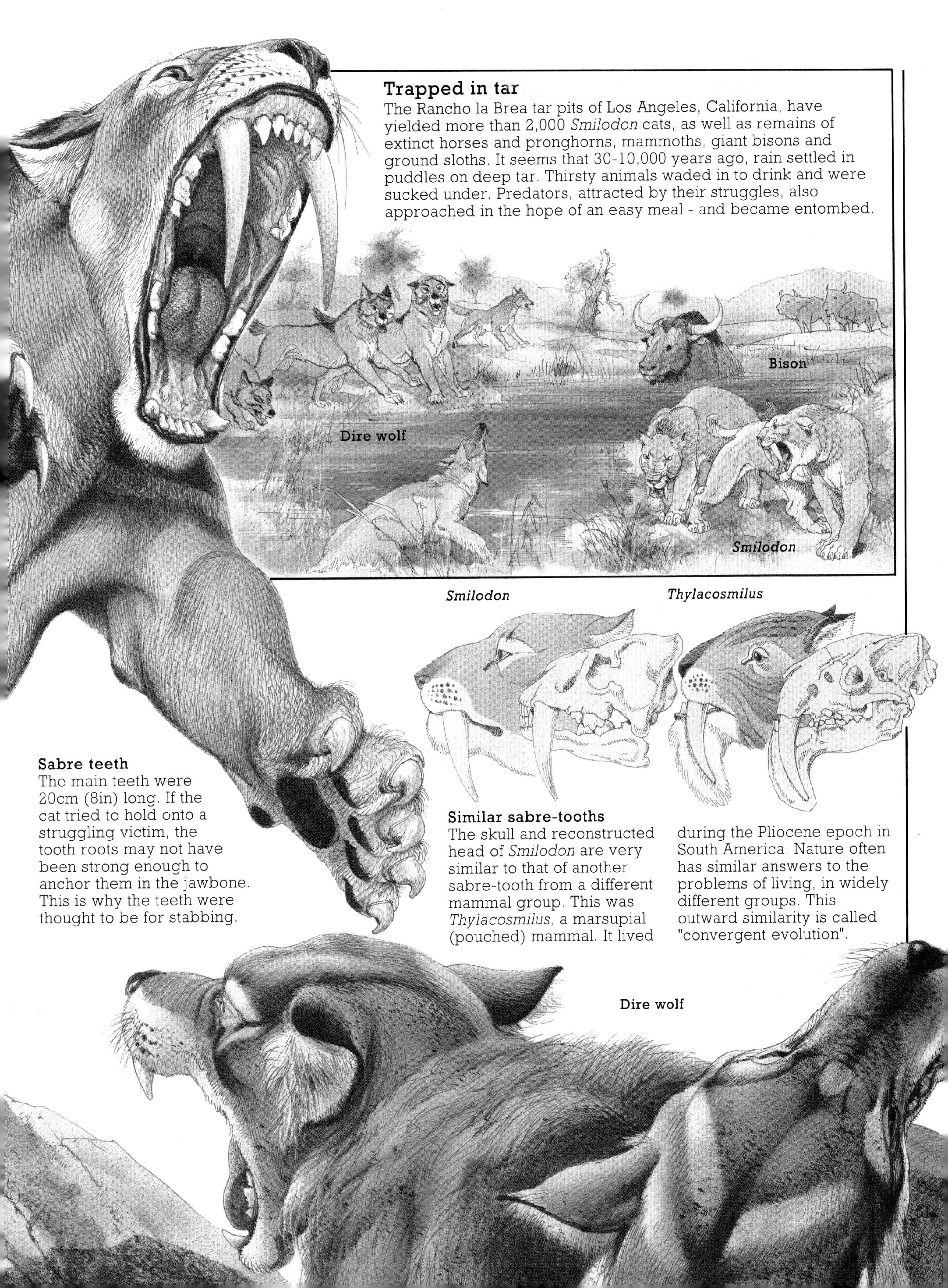

Trapped in tar

The Rancho la Brea tar pits of Los Angeles, California, have yielded more than 2,000 *Smilodon* cats, as well as remains of extinct horses and pronghorns, mammoths, giant bisons and ground sloths. It seems that 30-10,000 years ago, rain settled in puddles on deep tar. Thirsty animals waded in to drink and were sucked under. Predators, attracted by their struggles, also approached in the hope of an easy meal - and became entombed.

Sabre teeth

Thc main teeth were 20cm (8in) long. If the cat tried to hold onto a struggling victim, the tooth roots may not have been strong enough to anchor them in the jawbone. This is why the teeth were thought to be for stabbing.

Similar sabre-tooths

The skull and reconstructed head of *Smilodon* are very similar to that of another sabre-tooth from a different mammal group. This was *Thylacosmilus*, a marsupial (pouched) mammal. It lived during the Pliocene epoch in South America. Nature often has similar answers to the problems of living, in widely different groups. This outward similarity is called "convergent evolution".

EARLY HUMANS

There are four main kinds of apes. These are gibbons, orangutans, gorillas and chimpanzees. Biologists include humans with the apes in a group called the hominoids. Fossils show that other hominids have also appeared and became extinct over the past few million years. Some of these belonged to the hominids - the human and human-like family. Their fossils, along with other remains such as stone tools and ash-charred campfire sites, are evidence for the broad picture of how our own species, *Homo sapiens*, gradually evolved. We cannot say for sure that one kind of prehistoric human changed into the next. But knowing how nature works, this is far more likely than that new kinds of humans suddenly sprang up from nowhere.

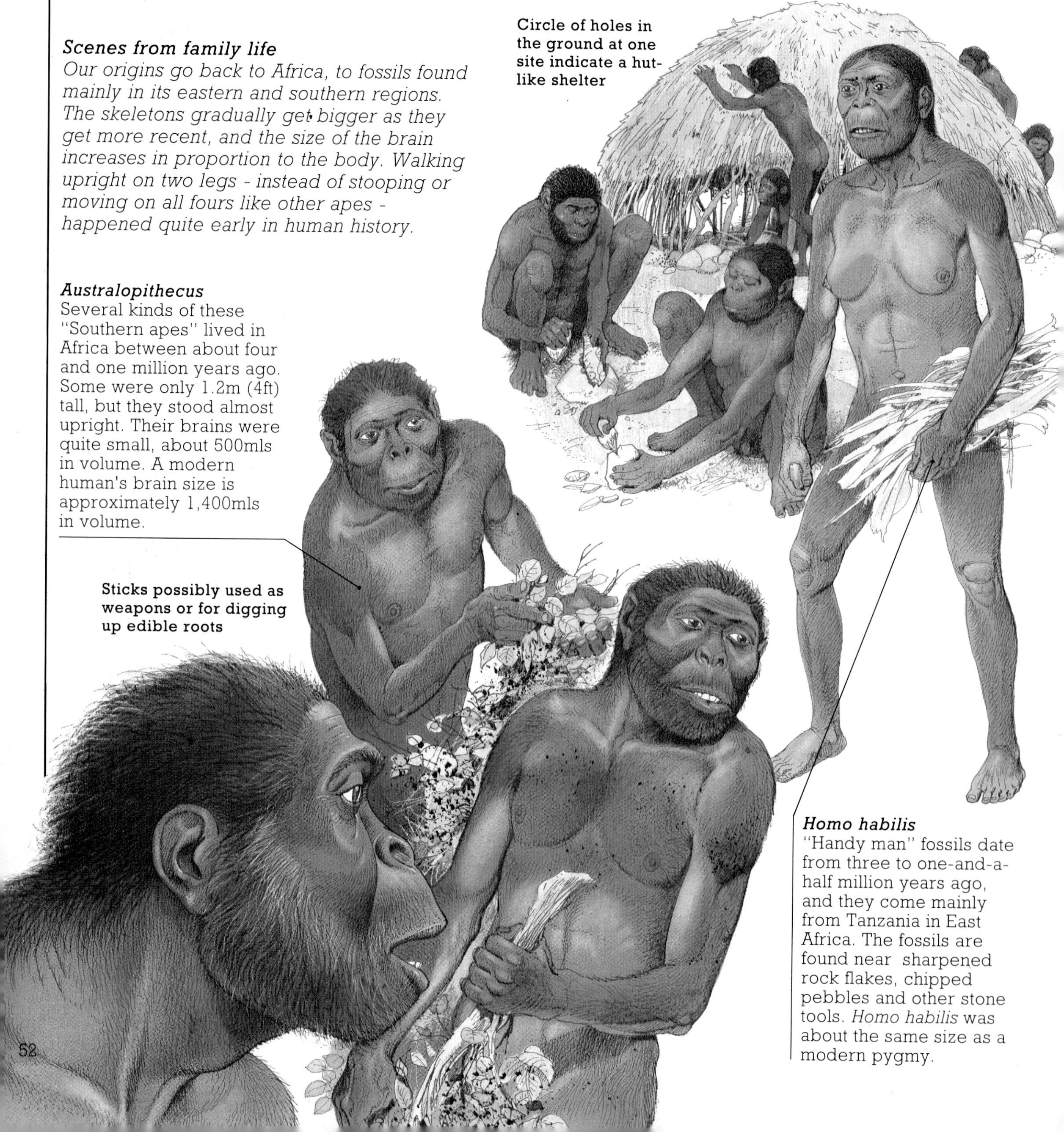

Scenes from family life
Our origins go back to Africa, to fossils found mainly in its eastern and southern regions. The skeletons gradually get bigger as they get more recent, and the size of the brain increases in proportion to the body. Walking upright on two legs - instead of stooping or moving on all fours like other apes - happened quite early in human history.

Circle of holes in the ground at one site indicate a hut-like shelter

Australopithecus
Several kinds of these "Southern apes" lived in Africa between about four and one million years ago. Some were only 1.2m (4ft) tall, but they stood almost upright. Their brains were quite small, about 500mls in volume. A modern human's brain size is approximately 1,400mls in volume.

Sticks possibly used as weapons or for digging up edible roots

Homo habilis
"Handy man" fossils date from three to one-and-a-half million years ago, and they come mainly from Tanzania in East Africa. The fossils are found near sharpened rock flakes, chipped pebbles and other stone tools. *Homo habilis* was about the same size as a modern pygmy.

The Neanderthalers

The fossils of these prehistoric humans were first found in Germany's Neander Valley. They lived from 120,000 to 40,000 years ago and were a subgroup, *Homo sapiens neanderthalensis*, of our own species. They were tall, strong and skilled in making stone and wood tools, ornaments, and clothing from animal hides.

Homo sapiens
"Wise man", our own species, began to appear less than half a million years ago. Gradually, they began to produce better tools and clothes, make beautiful paintings on cave walls, and hold ceremonies to bury the dead. Fully modern humans date from 40,000 years ago.

Homo erectus
"Upright man" remains have been found across Europe, Asia and Africa. These people lived from one-and-a-half million to 300,000 years ago. They were almost as tall as us, and they used fire for warmth, cooking and possibly defence.

END OF AN ERA

When a certain kind of animal or plant dies out and disappears for ever, we say that it has become extinct. Extinction, like the appearance of new species, is a natural part of evolution. It has been happening since life began on Earth. But at certain times in the past, many kinds of animals and plants became extinct together. Their fossils suddenly disappear from the rocks, to be replaced by new species over the following period. This sudden disappearance of many life forms is called a mass extinction, and it has happened many times during prehistory. The causes are not known. They may involve disease epidemics, climate changes, or events such as the explosion of a nearby star or a meteorite crashing into the Earth, which would alter the conditions for life.

Picking over the bones
Between 20,000 and 10,000 years ago, at the end of the Pleistocene epoch, many large animals became extinct: woolly mammoths, woolly rhinos, giant bison and ground sloths, deer and armadillos, sabre-toothed cats.... What was the cause?

Warmer weather?
Some of the mammals were very well suited to the intensely cold ice-age climate, with their thick fur and bulky bodies. Perhaps, as the weather warmed up, they could not evolve quickly enough.

A human cause?
Perhaps the wave of extinctions was linked to humans, who were spreading around the globe and rapidly improving their hunting methods. Could their "overkill" have edged these great creatures into extinction?

A worldwide problem?
Extinctions happened around the world, although chiefly in North and South America and Europe. Many mammals probably could not adapt to the changing conditions, but this did not apply to all the animals who disappeared.

At the end of the Permian

About 225 million years ago the greatest mass extinction of all time happened. Nine-tenths of the animal and plant species in the seas disappeared. They included all of the trilobites, some of which had survived a previous mass extinction at the end of the Devonian period, 120 million years before.

At the end of the Cretaceous

Some 64 million years ago, the dinosaurs suffered mass extinction They were not alone - sea reptiles like mosasaurs also died out, along with the flying pterosaurs. As well as the reptiles, about half of all sea-dwelling invertebrates disappeared, among them the ammonoids and microscopic foraminiferans.

Were humans there?
Previously it was believed that modern-type people arrived in North America only 15-12,000 years ago. This tied in well with the time of the extinctions. Yet today we have evidence of people in North America well before this time. This only adds to the puzzle.

Too-powerful weapons?
By 10,000 years ago, the stone and bone weapons made by people were deadly. Along with the superior cunning and teamwork of the human hunters, few prey could have survived.

What about today?
Since the late Pleistocene extinctions, new species have not appeared. In fact, animals and plants are now dying out faster than ever before. Humans are to blame for this. Estimates show that we are killing off one species every day.

REBUILDING THE PAST

The famous naturalist Charles Darwin, who suggested the idea of evolution by natural selection, pointed out that fossils give us a view of prehistoric life which is very limited. Because so many animals have soft, jelly-like bodies, these are hardly ever preserved as fossils. Of the others, only a tiny number die in conditions which suit fossilization. And of these, only a tiny number actually become fully-formed fossils. Even fewer are then found by people who actually know what they are! As we discover more fossils, and study them to rebuild the animals and plants as they were in life, we increase our knowledge of the prehistoric world. But it is still like looking at only a few parts of only a few of the pictures, from a very long movie film.

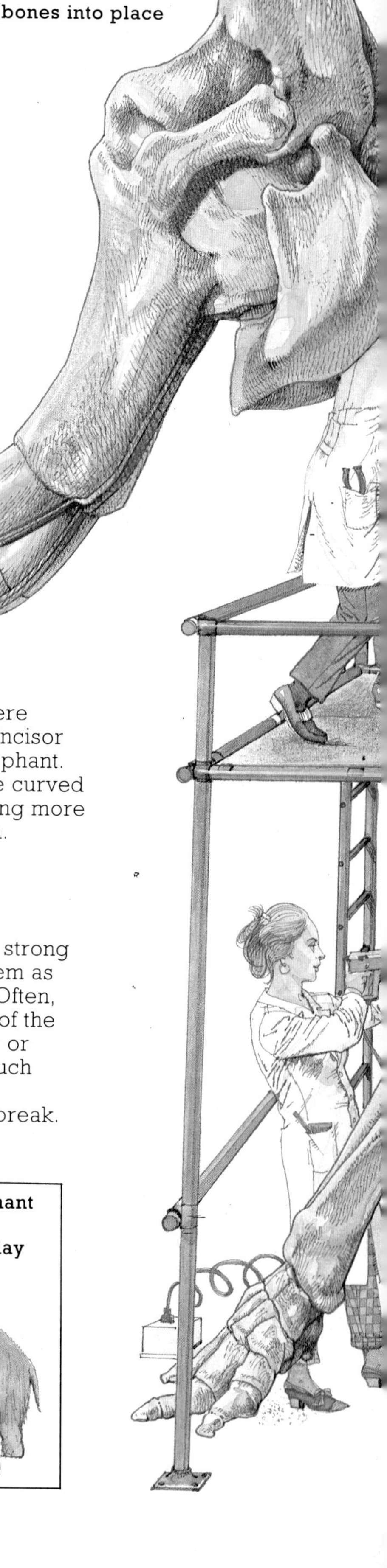

A series of pulleys is used to manoeuvre the bones into place

Bringing a mammoth back to life

The woolly mammoth died out thousands of years ago, but scientists have a good start when they are trying to reconstruct this creature. The bones are very similar to those of an animal that lives today - the elephant. They are also quite recent and are often in good condition for fossils, with few of them squashed or broken.

Tusks

The mammoth's tusks were enormously overgrown incisor teeth, as in a modern elephant. But they were even more curved and much longer, reaching more than 4.3m (14ft) in length.

Supporting frame

The heavy bones need a strong framework to support them as they are fitted together. Often, casts (copies) are made of the original bones, in plaster or glass-fibre. These are much lighter, and they can be replaced if they fall and break.

Finding the bones

Mammoth bones are very large, so they are not difficult to find and identify. But their size makes them a problem, since when they have become stone, they weigh several tonnes. Cranes and lifting gear must be brought to the site, and specially reinforced trucks are needed to carry the fossils away over rough ground. Sometimes they are even airlifted out by helicopter!

1 *Moeritherium*, an elephant of 35 million years ago
2 African elephant of today
3 Steppe mammoth

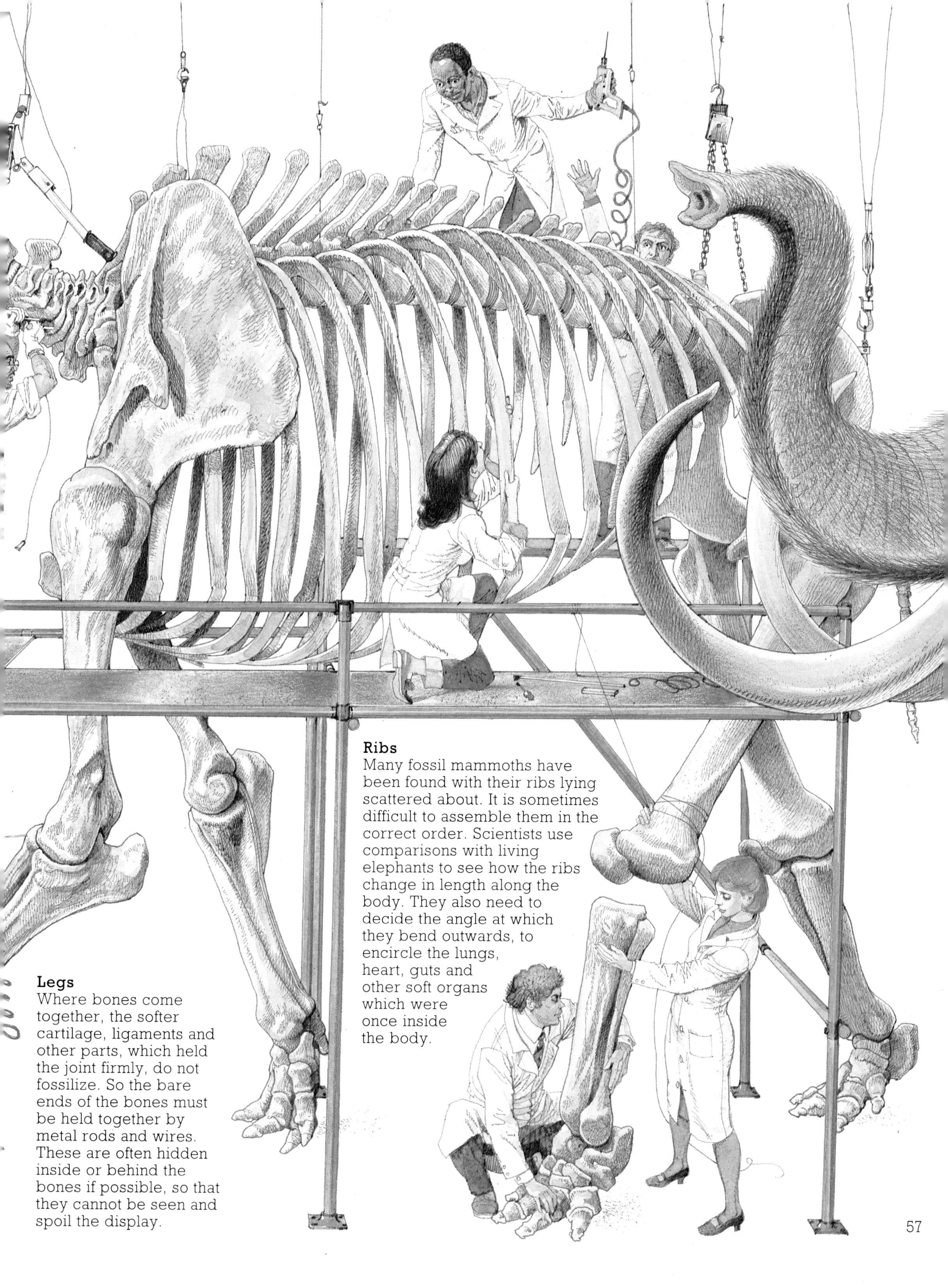

Ribs
Many fossil mammoths have been found with their ribs lying scattered about. It is sometimes difficult to assemble them in the correct order. Scientists use comparisons with living elephants to see how the ribs change in length along the body. They also need to decide the angle at which they bend outwards, to encircle the lungs, heart, guts and other soft organs which were once inside the body.

Legs
Where bones come together, the softer cartilage, ligaments and other parts, which held the joint firmly, do not fossilize. So the bare ends of the bones must be held together by metal rods and wires. These are often hidden inside or behind the bones if possible, so that they cannot be seen and spoil the display.

Cutting teeth
Earlier relatives of the mammoths had tusks on their lower jaw. They ground their food by moving the jaws in a circular fashion. Mammoths, like the elephants of today, had only two tusks in the upper jaw.

Long fur coat
Woolly mammoths lived through Ice Ages and their long, woolly fur gave good protection against the intense cold. Frozen bodies show that the fur was reddish-brown in colour, with a scattering of longer, tougher, thicker, darker "guard hairs".

Baby frozen stiff
In 1977 scientists found a baby mammoth that had been less than a year old when alive, frozen solid in Siberia. The mammoth died around 40,000 years ago and the flesh is so well preserved that, when thawed, some has been eaten by wild animals, and even by sled dogs.

Flesh on bones

When it comes to putting flesh, muscles and skin on the fossilized bones, scientists have another great advantage with mammoths. Several almost complete woolly mammoths have been found "deep-frozen" in the ice of Alaska and Siberia. These remains tell us the animal's type of fur and even its colour.

Things can go wrong . . .

In 1840, large fossil bones were found in the Missouri River area of the USA which were reassembled into a large, mammoth-like creature. In fact there were two sets of bones from two creatures and the reconstruction had several extra pairs of ribs. It was thought to be aquatic, with webbed feet. One artist even pictured it hanging from a branch by its "horns" when asleep! The horns were really mammoth tusks, put on upside down. The animal was called the Missouri Leviathan, after the ocean-living monster of the Bible.

Mammuthus trogontherii **was probably the first mammoth to develop a hairy coat to protect it against the cold**

Footprints

Like the mammoths themselves, many mammoth footprints have been found frozen into mud and fossilized. The size of the print shows how big the animal was, while the distance between each track reveals the length of its stride. It also shows whether the mammoth had been walking or running. Similar prints from other prehistoric animals, including dinosaurs, help us to work out how heavy they were and how fast they were able to run.

A record is made of the size of the print

Photographs are taken from several angles

"LIVING FOSSILS"

Some kinds of animals and plants did not survive on Earth for long. They either died out soon after they appeared, or they evolved into new forms. Certain kinds of animals have been around for millions of years - if not as exactly the same species alive today, then as very similar ones. When scientists call such animals "primitive", this means that they or their group appeared a very long time ago. Being primitive does not mean being out-of-date or poorly designed. On the contrary, some primitive designs, such as sharks, are still around because they are efficient. In other cases, fossils show that a group which was once varied and numerous - such as the rhinos - has slowly become smaller and less numerous. So they are also primitive, but now less successful. These types of animals could not evolve to keep up with changing conditions.

The "Living Fossil Zoo"

Imagine walking through a zoo of "Living Fossils". Many such animals differ at least slightly from their fossil relatives, while others have evolved only recently to resemble long-gone species.

Rhinos
From about 40 to two million years ago, there were dozens of rhino species. Some were bigger than elephants, others as small as pigs. Not all had horns. Yet only five species survive, all now very rare.

Dingoes
A close relative of the domestic dog, the dingo is thought to have been in Australia for at least 10,000 years. It may have arrived with some of the Aboriginal people, as a guard dog or to help with tracking. Wild dingoes attack farm animals and are pests in some areas.

Elephants
Like rhinos, the elephants were once widespread and numerous, with many different species. Even less than two million years ago they varied from huge imperial mammoths to pygmy elephants almost as small as sheep. Today only two species remain, the African and Asian.

Trees
Fossils of some flowering (blossom) trees appeared 100 million years ago (pages 40-41). Magnolias were one of the earliest. The gingkos or maidenhair trees, related to conifers, were common and widespread 150 million years ago. Today the one remaining species, *Gingko biloba*, is strikingly similar to the first fossil forms.

Hoatzin
This curious bird from the Amazon riverbanks is a poor flier. Young hoatzins have two hook-like claws at the front of each wing, rather like *Archaeopteryx* (pages 42-43). These may not be evolutionary "leftovers", but newer adaptations to tree life.

Tree shrews
The tree shrews of the rainforests of South East Asia are not true shrews (and neither do they all live in trees). There is much debate about their origin. They probably evolved as a separate group very early in the history of mammals.

Back to the sea

Life first appeared in the sea, and so an aquarium would show present-day animals with the longest evolutionary history. One of the best contenders for the title "oldest living fossil" is the lampshell (brachiopod) group. These creatures are protected by a shell which has two halves, held together by a strong muscle. There are about 260 species alive today, in seas around the world. Yet more than 30,000 fossil species have been discovered, stretching back to early Cambrian times.

Coelacanths

Discovered by scientists in 1938, the living coelacanth caused a sensation. The first fossils of this 1.8m (6ft) lobe-finned fish are more than 350 million years old, and they disappear from the fossil record 70 million years ago - or so it was thought!

Tuatara

The tuatara is not a lizard, but the only remaining member of the reptile group Rhynchocephalia, which flourished before the dinosaurs (page 22). It now lives on only a few islands off New Zealand.

Sharks
One of the most successful and long-lasting of all animal groups, the sharks date from Devonian times (page 16). The skeleton is made of gristly cartilage, which is rarely preserved. The only body parts that regularly form fossils are the scales and teeth, which are hardened by minerals.

Gila monsters
Only two of the 3,000 lizard species are poisonous - the Mexican beaded lizard and the Gila monster, both from south-west and southern North America. The lizard group is 230 million years old and once included the fearsome sea-dwelling mosasaurs from the Age of Dinosaurs.

Underwater relics
Some 210 million years ago, turtles very like those of today swam in Triassic waters. Sea-pens, relatives of anemones, crowded the sea bed 400 million years before them. Lampshell shells were some of the very first hard animal structures to turn to fossils, more than 550 million years ago.

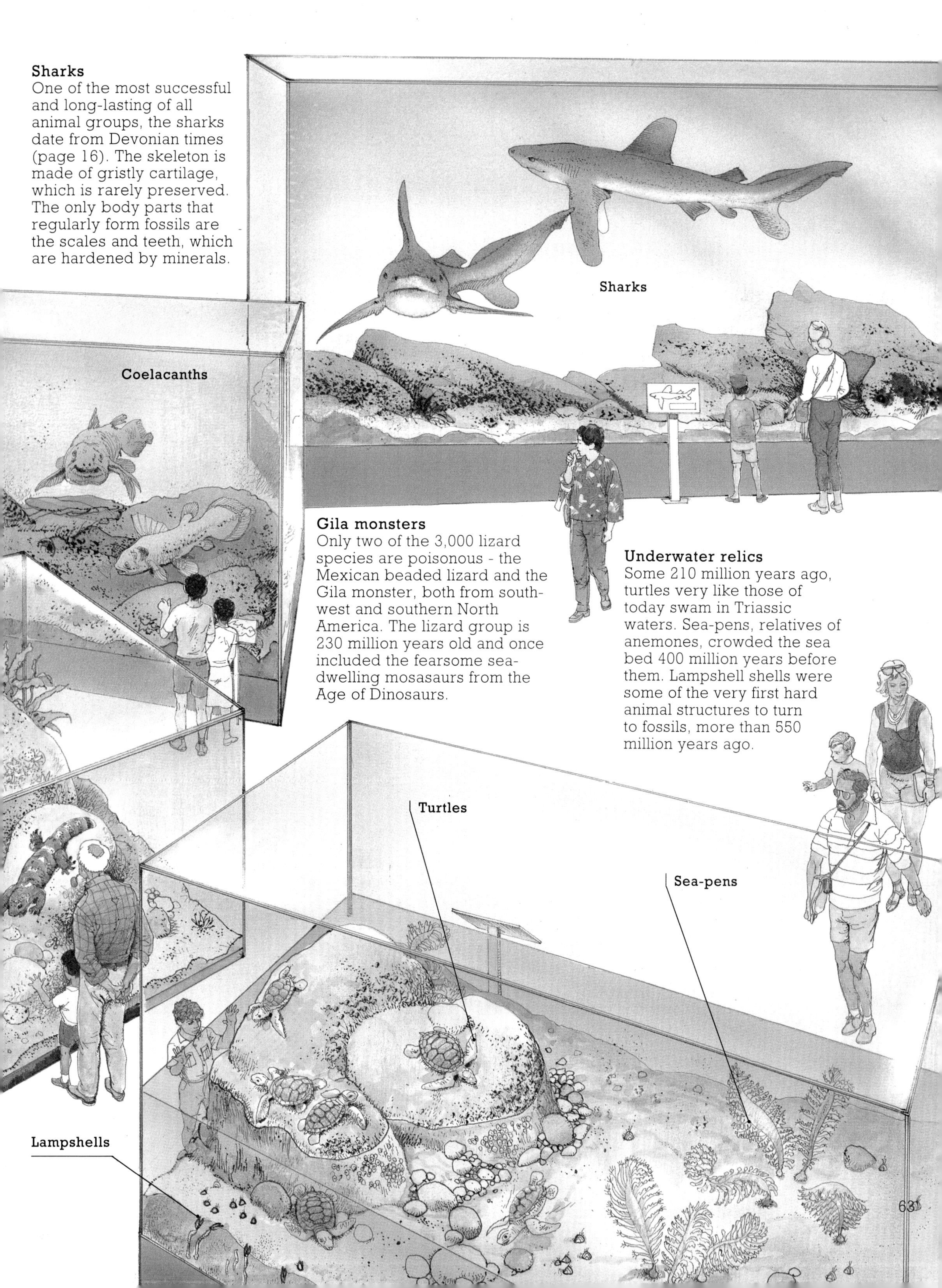

INDEX